S0-ACB-913

Sydney

WORLD BIBLIOGRAPHICAL SERIES

General Editors:
Robert G. Neville (Executive Editor)
John J. Horton

Robert A. Myers   Hans H. Wellisch
Ian Wallace   Ralph Lee Woodward, Jr.

John J. Horton is Deputy Librarian of the University of Bradford and was formerly Chairman of its Academic Board of Studies in Social Sciences. He has maintained a longstanding interest in the discipline of area studies and its associated bibliographical problems, with special reference to European Studies. In particular he has published in the field of Icelandic and of Yugoslav studies, including the two relevant volumes in the World Bibliographical Series.

Robert A. Myers is Associate Professor of Anthropology in the Division of Social Sciences and Director of Study Abroad Programs at Alfred University, Alfred, New York. He has studied post-colonial island nations of the Caribbean and has spent two years in Nigeria on a Fulbright Lectureship. His interests include international public health, historical anthropology and developing societies. In addition to *Amerindians of the Lesser Antilles: a bibliography* (1981), *A Resource Guide to Dominica, 1493-1986* (1987) and numerous articles, he has compiled the World Bibliographical Series volumes on *Dominica* (1987), *Nigeria* (1989) and *Ghana* (1991).

Ian Wallace is Professor of German at the University of Bath. A graduate of Oxford in French and German, he also studied in Tübingen, Heidelberg and Lausanne before taking teaching posts at universities in the USA, Scotland and England. He specializes in contemporary German affairs, especially literature and culture, on which he has published numerous articles and books. In 1979 he founded the journal *GDR Monitor*, which he continues to edit under its new title *German Monitor*.

Hans H. Wellisch is Professor emeritus at the College of Library and Information Services, University of Maryland. He was President of the American Society of Indexers and was a member of the International Federation for Documentation. He is the author of numerous articles and several books on indexing and abstracting, and has published *The Conversion of Scripts and Indexing and Abstracting: an International Bibliography*, and *Indexing from A to Z*. He also contributes frequently to *Journal of the American Society for Information Science*, *The Indexer* and other professional journals.

Ralph Lee Woodward, Jr. is Director of Graduate Studies at Tulane University, New Orleans. He is the author of *Central America, a Nation Divided*, 2nd ed. (1985), as well as several monographs and more than seventy scholarly articles on modern Latin America. He has also compiled volumes in the World Bibliographical Series on *Belize* (1980), *El Salvador* (1988), *Guatemala* (Rev. Ed.) (1992) and *Nicaragua* (Rev. Ed.) (1994). Dr. Woodward edited the Central American section of the *Research Guide to Central America and the Caribbean* (1985) and is currently associate editor of Scribner's *Encyclopedia of Latin American History*.

VOLUME 223

Sydney

I. Kepars

Compiler

CLIO PRESS

OXFORD, ENGLAND · SANTA BARBARA, CALIFORNIA
DENVER, COLORADO

DU
178
.K44
2000

© Copyright 2000 by ABC-CLIO Ltd.

British Library Cataloguing in Publication Data

Kepars, I.
Sydney. – (World bibliographical series; v. 223)
1. Sydney (N. S. W.) – Bibliography
I. Title
016.9'9441

ISBN 1–85109–328–1

ABC-CLIO Ltd.,
Old Clarendon Ironworks,
35A Great Clarendon Street,
Oxford OX2 6AT, England.

————————

ABC-CLIO Inc.,
130 Cremona Drive,
Santa Barbara,
CA 93117, USA

Designed by Bernard Crossland.
Typeset by ABC-CLIO Ltd., Oxford, England.
Printed and bound in Great Britain by print in black, Midsomer Norton.

THE WORLD BIBLIOGRAPHICAL SERIES

This series, which is principally designed for the English speaker, will eventually cover every country (and some of the world's principal regions and cities), each in a separate volume comprising annotated entries on works dealing with its history, geography, economy and politics; and with its people, their culture, customs, religion and social organization. Attention will also be paid to current living conditions – housing, education, newspapers, clothing, etc. – that are all too often ignored in standard bibliographies; and to those particular aspects relevant to individual countries. Each volume seeks to achieve, by use of careful selectivity and critical assessment of the literature, an expression of the country and an appreciation of its nature and national aspirations, to guide the reader towards an understanding of its importance. The keynote of the series is to provide, in a uniform format, an interpretation of each country that will express its culture, its place in the world, and the qualities and background that make it unique. The views expressed in individual volumes, however, are not necessarily those of the publisher.

VOLUMES IN THE SERIES

Contents

Contents

Contents

Introduction

Sydney, the capital of New South Wales, the eastern-most of the six states and two territories which make up the Commonwealth of Australia, is the oldest, largest and most cosmopolitan city in the country. It was founded as a convict settlement by Captain Arthur Phillip. Captain Phillip had landed his fleet in Botany Bay, but finding the surrounding area unsuitable, explored northwards and on 26 January 1788 sailed into the great waters of Port Jackson, now popularly known as Sydney Harbour. He named Sydney Cove, the first European settlement on the continent, after Lord Sydney, Secretary of the Home Office in London.

Geography

Sydney is situated on Australia's populous east coast about 870 kilometres north of Melbourne, the capital of Victoria, and almost 1,000 kilometres south of Brisbane, the capital of Queensland. Sydney lies 16,200 kilometres southeast of Rome (a twenty-three-hour flight), 12,000 kilometres southwest of Los Angeles (a thirteen-hour flight), 7,400 kilometres south of Tokyo (a nine-and-a-half-hour flight) and 1,360 kilometres west of Auckland, New Zealand (a three-hour flight). The city is built around the harbour of Port Jackson, but the Sydney metropolitan area sprawls over 1,800 square kilometres and stretches south to the foothills of the Southern Tablelands, west to the rise of the Blue Mountains and in the north to the fringes of the great national parks near Broken Bay. The terrain is hilly and the physical layout spectacular, due to the harbour's numerous bays and headlands. The city is built on a vast sandstone plateau, reaching an elevation of 150 metres in the south and up to 210 metres at the city's northern extremities. These uplands are deeply trenched by streams draining to Broken Bay, Port Jackson, Botany Bay and Port Hacking.

The physical geography which decided the choice of the original settlement has paid great dividends for modern Sydney. Port Jackson, noted for its beauty, is an all-important recreational area for Sydneysiders. From Barranjoey on Broken Bay in the north, to Cronulla on Port Hacking in the south, the coastline stretches for some 70 kilometres in a series of jutting, scrub-covered sandstone headlands, alternating with crescent-shaped beaches. These are famous for being public and providing world-beating surfing within easy reach of most of Sydney's inhabitants.

Sydney seasons are opposite to those in the Northern Hemisphere. At Christmas time it is hot, while July and August are the coldest months. Summer begins in December, autumn in March, winter in June and spring in September. With only twenty-three days without sunshine per year, Sydney boasts a quasi-tropical climate. The summer mean temperature hovers around 25°C and in winter drops to about 12°C. Means, of course, do not tell the full story. During the hot summer spells temperatures can hit 40°C and combined with high humidity the climatic conditions may become quite oppressive. Average monthly rainfall ranges from 75 to 130 mm and torrential downpours are inevitable between October and March, often causing flash floods. Climatic extremes are not uncommon. During the dry summer of 1993/94 fires swept from the surrounding forest areas into the suburbs of metropolitan Sydney causing loss of lives and property, while during the winter months of June to August, far western suburbs near the Blue Mountains consistently record below-zero morning temperatures.

In common with other big cities of the world, traffic congestion and atmospheric and water pollution are real problems in Sydney. There is great concern about harbour and ocean beaches, especially after heavy rainfall, when billions of litres of rubbish and untreated effluents emerge from overflow points. In addition, millions of litres of nearly raw sewage mixed with toxic industrial waste are pumped out into the ocean daily, which, in unfavourable wind and tidal conditions, get washed back onto the beaches. Aircraft noise from Sydney's international Kingsford Smith Airport, situated among residential suburbs, has become a major issue for nearby residents. The government has tried to reduce the level of noise in the worst affected areas by 'spreading' the flight paths.

Flora and fauna

When the British first saw the Sydney landscape in 1788, they were staggered by its strangeness. Not only were seasons out of phase, with winter falling in June and summer in December, but native wildflowers bloomed throughout the year with the brightest displays during the winter months, when the wattles transformed the bush into a brilliant chrome yellow. Instead of walking on all fours, the animals hopped about; brightly coloured birds made sounds strange to European ears and the trees shed bark instead of leaves. The strangest were the marsupials, which produced imperfectly formed offspring and suckled them in their pouches. These included the wombat, the possum, the kangaroo and the koala, the latter resembling a small bear, sleeping during the day and feeding on eucalyptus leaves at night. Even more puzzling was the platypus – an amphibious creature with fur, a duck-like bill and webbed feet, which laid eggs and suckled its young. Besides these benign creatures the bush held dangerous surprises – poisonous snakes and deadly spiders – while man-eating sharks cruised the waters of Sydney Harbour.

Many of these native animals and birds, especially wallabies, kangaroos, possums, koalas, parrots, cockatoos and kookaburras can still be seen in the wild around the city outskirts or in the reserves which today total about 5,700 hectares in the metropolitan area. Two large national parks north and south of the city – Ku-ring-gai Chase of 16,200 hectares and the Royal National Park of 13,800 hectares – abound with native flora and fauna. Likewise, over 100 species of reptiles live in the Sydney region, but these are shy creatures and seldom observed.

Swimming beaches in the Harbour and on the ocean shores are safety-netted against sharks and there has not been a fatality in decades. Australian flora and fauna can be observed in its fullness at the Royal Botanic Gardens and Taronga Park Zoo, conveniently situated a short ferry ride away from the Central Business District. In August 1999 a sperm whale frolicked in Sydney Harbour for two weeks and caught the imagination of Sydneysiders. This may become a much more common sight; since the world-wide ban on whale hunting, whales have begun migrating up the east coast of Australia to breed in the warm waters off Queensland. Concern has been expressed about whale interference with the Olympic yachting events, which are to be held on the Harbour in September 2000.

The people

Sydney has a population of 4 million out of the Australian total of 19 million. Although a greater proportion of Sydneysiders than other Australians reside in high-density accommodation such as apartments and town houses, most still prefer life in a detached house on a quarter-acre block in the suburbs. Thus, although in terms of population Sydney ranks amongst the mid-fifty cities in the world, it takes up more space than Tokyo, the largest, with its 26.5 million people. Sydney encompasses an urban area six times that of Rome, which has a population of only one million fewer inhabitants.

For a long time, the Anglo-Irish conflict, transported to the Antipodes by the many Irish political prisoners amongst the early convicts, influenced and shaped the emerging Australian national character. Segregated in special camps to minimize their suspected rebelliousness, the Irish were able to retain a separate identity through their common language, religion and political beliefs. In March 1804 their anti-authoritarian stance culminated in the Castle Hill Rising, which was cruelly suppressed by the military and free settler volunteers. From then on, the Irish bushranger, or highway robber, who terrorized the early settlers, became the stuff of legends in the popular mind, immortalized by folk ballads. The image of the larrikin for a long time was considered as the archetypal Australian figure: 'the Aussie'. True or false, this anti-hero image still holds and was reinforced in the character of Crocodile Dundee, the hero of the popular film of the same name.

Once granted a ticket of leave, ex-convicts were free to engage in any lawful occupation for their own advantage. Many, including former political prisoners, succeeded in establishing careers in business and commerce and became some of the most affluent individuals in Sydney's society, yet were still snubbed by the Anglo-Australian establishment.

The Second World War period brought an end to Australia's isolation from the rest of the world. Advancing transport and communication technologies gradually helped to reduce the long-standing 'tyranny of distance' between Australia and the rest of the world, but a more profound shift in the national ethos was caused by new population movements. Firstly, the American servicemen, who were stationed in Sydney during the war years in great numbers, introduced a different, more dynamic lifestyle to the city. This was followed by the influx of a new breed of immigrants from war-ravaged Europe, which forever changed the prevailing Anglo-Saxon culture of Sydney. Today, one in three Sydneysiders, or well over one million people, were born overseas or are first-generation immigrants representing over 150 nationalities. Census figures show an unprecedented change in the population make up: while more immigrants are settling in Sydney than in any other city of the country, the Australian born residents appear to be leaving. Between 1991 and 1996 censuses, the native population grew by only 1.9 per cent, or five times slower than the immigrant intake.

History

The ancestors of the Aborigines of the Sydney region had migrated to the Australian continent some 50,000 years ago. At the time when the first European settlers arrived there were approximately 3,000 Aborigines living in the Sydney region speaking three different languages. Their tribal social order had developed an intricate and sophisticated cultural life expressed in complex ceremonies. The surrounding bushland and tidal waters provided plentiful food resources and a harmonious interaction with the physical environment manifested itself in a mystic relationship with the land.

The English arrived on 16 January 1788 in what is now known as the First Fleet, consisting of eleven ships. When every person had landed the settlement amounted to 1,030 people, comprising the Governor Arthur Phillip, his staff of 9, the surveyor-general, the surgeon and 4 assistants, the chaplain and his wife, 2 servants, 211 marines, 27 wives of marines, 19 children of marines, 736 convicts and 17 children of convicts. This was the beginning of the European history of Sydney.

The seeds of conflict with the Aborigines were sown early and ended in a harvest of catastrophes. Within the next eighty years all of the indigenous population were dead, exterminated either directly by the invading settlers, killed by European diseases or perishing through the reckless destruction of the environment which had supported their tribal lifestyle. Meanwhile, faced with the unfamiliar environment and harsh climatic extremes, the new settlers experienced early crop failures and resulting hunger. The plentiful native food resources in the surrounding bushland, which had so richly supported the local Aboriginal tribes, were never utilized, perhaps out of feelings of white supremacy. Instead, survival depended on the arrival of each new convict fleet and the supplies it carried from England. Semi-starvation was aggravated by the newly developed hostility of the Aborigines, who, once they realized that the new arrivals were to stay at the expense of the original inhabitants, began a campaign of resistance.

The wretched living conditions, water shortages, chronic drought and food rationing, increased drunkenness and deteriorating moral standards gave short shrift to Governor Phillip's original plan of creating a prosperous colony of the British Empire where free settlers, together with worthy emancipists, would work the land using convict slave labour. In 1792 Captain Phillip returned to England, a broken man.

The running of the fledgling community was taken over by Major Francis Grose, the Lieutenant-Governor and commander of the New South Wales Corps. Soon all the important official positions were filled by military personnel who freely appropriated newly arrived supplies and operated a trade monopoly. Rum became the universal barter and the New South Wales Corps was popularly known as 'the Rum Corps'. From 1792 to 1810 the Rum Corps effectively ran the colony for their own benefit, overpowering Governor Hunter and in 1808 arresting Governor Bligh during the so-called Rum Rebellion. The tradition of crime and shady dealings at the highest levels became endemic in the fabric of New South Wales administration, and as recently as the 1980s and 1990s several parliamentary enquiries exposed corruption and participation in organized criminal activities up to police commissioner and ministerial level.

The growing power of the Rum Corps caused concern to the authorities in London. In 1810 they despatched Major-General Lachlan Macquarie with his own regiment to take control as Governor. The next eleven years, when

Sydney flourished, have been named by historians 'the Age of Macquarie'. From the day of his arrival Macquarie set out to develop Sydney and its surroundings into a model colony. He issued a series of regulations for widening and straightening the streets and embarked on an ambitious building programme under the supervision of convict architect Francis Greenway. Some of these structures, such as St. James Church, the Hyde Park Barracks and the original Rum Hospital, have survived to this day. The Bank of New South Wales (now Westpac) was founded, as was a civilian police force. The population increased rapidly and land under cultivation in the Sydney area grew fourfold during the Macquarie era.

Macquarie's grand vision was perceived by the English authorities in London as an extravagance for a convict settlement, as were his programmes of convict emancipation and liberalization. These were also opposed by the colonial establishment who desired large land grants and did not want to lose cheap convict labour. In 1821 Macquarie was replaced. Discredited, he left Sydney and died in poverty in London in 1824.

During the following decades, under Governors Brisbane, Darling, Bourke and Gipps, trade and business boomed and Sydney continued to expand. By 1841 the population had increased to 30,000. With the growth of exports from the surrounding country areas, prosperity increased and Sydney was shedding its image of an urban gaol. In 1824 a Legislative Council was appointed and in 1826 a public library was established. The colony's first free press came into being with the publication of the *Sydney Morning Herald* in April 1831. In 1840 the transportation of convicts ended and two years later *An Act to declare the Town of Sydney to be a City and to incorporate that Inhabitants thereof...* was passed. The City of Sydney was a now self-governed, if still a rough and often unruly, place. Social problems were aggravated by widespread drinking in the numerous taverns and illegal drinking dens and prostitution. Crime and vice were rampant in certain parts of the town and those who could afford it began to move to the outer periphery. The first residential suburbs of Double Bay, St Leonards and Elizabeth Bay came into being.

The large quantities of gold found near Bathurst in 1851, some 200 kilometres west of Sydney across the Blue Mountains, and the consequent gold rush, drew a lot of people from all over the world to Sydney. Although Sydney's population nearly doubled in the 1850s, from 54,000 to 96,000 inhabitants, most of the larger gold discoveries were in Victoria. Its capital Melbourne boomed and became the largest city in Australia, which it remained until the depression of the 1890s.

During the second half of the 19th century Sydney was characterized by great expansion. As trading grew the Stock Exchange was opened; in the mid-1850s Sydney University was established and in 1855 the first train ran between Sydney and Parramatta. Until the 1880s, when tramways were introduced, Sydney was still a 'walking distance' city, with most people living near their place of employment. The expanding public transport network enabled the new middle classes to leave the deteriorating living conditions of the inner city with its rapidly growing industrialization and to move to the new suburbs. The ever expanding Sydney urban sprawl, with its 'house on a quarter of an acre block' per family, was under way and has continued to the present. Meanwhile, the inner areas of Sydney turned into slums, populated by the working-class poor. Appalling sanitary conditions, coupled with overcrowding, caused a number of epidemics, culminating in the 1900 bubonic plague. Although only 303 cases and 103 deaths were officially reported, the plague caused widespread social and economic disruption and profoundly affected the lives of thousands of Sydneysiders. Urged by general fear of 'contamination', the authorities began large-scale slum clearances in the inner areas of Sydney as well as some reforms of the public health system.

The Federation movement of the late 19th century culminated in the creation of the Commonwealth of Australia on 1 January 1901. The colony of New South Wales became a state and Sydney its capital with a population of 480,000 people.

During the early part of the 20th century Sydney's public transport system continued to expand and an underground electric city rail line began operations to the Eastern suburbs. Plans were made for a major harbour crossing, which culminated in 1932 with the opening of the Sydney Harbour Bridge – for a long time the city's best known icon. The northern side of the harbour, which until then had been accessible only by ferry services, was opened up for rapid commercial and residential growth. By the turn of the century Sydney's population growth, sustained by new development in the manufacturing industries, overtook that of Melbourne and it has remained Australia's largest city until the present.

In 1942, during the Second World War, Japanese midget submarines penetrated into Sydney Harbour, sank a small vessel and fired a few shells into the suburbs of Bondi and Rose Bay. Yet the most lasting effect of the war on Sydney was the attack on Australia's English-style social norms brought about by the American military presence in the city. The Americanization of Sydneysiders' lifestyles was reinforced during the Vietnam War years, when Sydney became an R&R (rest and recreation) base for American GIs on leave from the war zone. The Kings Cross area, always the most bohemian of Sydney's suburbs, became the entertainment centre for the soldiers. As the Asian conflict dragged on and conscription was introduced to swell the ranks of the Australian troops in Vietnam, Sydney witnessed major civil unrest with streets blocked on several occasions by large numbers of protesters against Australian involvement in the conflict.

Introduction

The American influence was counteracted by the large-scale post-war immigration programmes which brought great numbers of Europeans to Sydney. With the shedding of its infamous 'White Australia' policy, Australia opened its doors to the Vietnamese refugees and other Asian immigrants soon followed. Sydney was fast becoming a cosmopolitan city.

The physical appearance of the city was rapidly being altered by the demolition of many old, beautiful and historically significant buildings, which were replaced by monotonous high-rise skyscrapers. During the 1970s, the militant Builders Labourers Federation, supported by many middle-class activists, created a unique, world-first alliance and introduced the device of the 'green ban', derived from the old trade union tactic of the 'black ban' on construction work by its members. This action stopped an estimated $4000 million worth in construction projects on Sydney's parklands, historic sites and low-cost residential areas. Due to this pressure, the New South Wales government in 1977 created the Heritage Council of New South Wales, charged with the conservation of both the natural and built environment. Today, the effect of the green bans can be enjoyed in the restored historical areas of the Rocks and Woolloomooloo and elsewhere in Sydney.

Sydney's most spectacular and most controversial building of the post-war period is the Sydney Opera House. A venue for the performing arts, it was originally designed by the Danish architect Joern Utzon in 1957. After much political infighting and controversy it opened in 1973. With its sail-like roof, covered in white ceramic tiles suggestive of the yachts that sail round it on Sydney Harbour, it is one of the great examples of modern architecture in the world and vies with the Sydney Harbour Bridge as a symbol of Sydney. The construction boom of the 1970s and 1980s bequeathed other large-scale tourist developments to Sydney, such as Darling Harbour and the Rocks area. In the 1990s another Harbour crossing, in the form of a tunnel adjacent to the Harbour Bridge, came into operation. Manufacturing industry, which boomed in the immediate post-war period, has gradually given way to tertiary industries, like finance, communications and services and Sydney is the Australian headquarters for many international firms, especially in the mining, computing and banking industries. The early 1990s saw a slump in construction and the general economy which is now recovering, partly due to large-scale construction projects associated with the Olympic Games in September 2000.

Sydney today

Today Sydney is the biggest city in Australia, ten times the size of the nation's capital Canberra and twenty-five per cent bigger than Melbourne, its perennial cultural rival. Not only is Sydney the financial and cultural capital of Australia, but it also has a superbly beautiful physical environment which no other city in Australia and very few in the world can equal.

Sydney Harbour, or Port Jackson as it was originally named, which permeates the built environment, provides some of the more exciting aspects to life in Sydney. Much of the 240 kilometres of foreshore retains its natural bushland with parks, walking tracks, beaches and picnic spots, providing magnificent recreational areas for locals and visitors alike. A harbour ferry service offers an efficient transport network to waterside areas. Visitors are encouraged to make trips to Manly on the ocean, Watson's Bay near the South Heads of the harbour entrance and Parramatta River, an estuary of the harbour. These are never-to-be-forgotten experiences.

With over thirty kilometres of sandy beaches within easy reach of the city, a beach culture flourishes with 'bronzed Aussies' of all sexes seeking sun and surf during Sydney's long summers. With an incidence of skin cancer which is the highest in the world, the 'bronzed' image has taken a beating in recent years and most beachgoers these days cover up. Bondi and Manly beaches should be visited and experienced by all sun-loving tourists.

Sydney is also renowned for its cosmopolitan character. It is home to a large gay community, estimated at some 400,000 individuals. Every February/March the government encourages the biggest celebration of homosexuality in the world – the Sydney Gay and Lesbian Mardi Gras, which attracts a large number of overseas visitors and local spectators.

Sydney is a successful multicultural community, with an ethnic mix rivalled only by New York and Tel Aviv. Approximately one quarter of Sydney's households speak a language other than English at home. The most common non-English languages are Chinese (ten per cent) and Italian (ten per cent). The combination of cultural, ethnic and environmental diversity has created a magnificent tourist destination. Over six million tourists visit Sydney every year. On several occasions the readers of the British Conde Nast *Traveller* magazine have voted Sydney the best foreign city in the world, and it is always placed among the top ten for all categories, such as food, fun, location and friendliness. The members of various other organizations, such as *Travel & Leisure* magazine, American Express and International Congress and Convention Association, have made similar acknowledgements.

In common with other large cities of the world, Sydney has its downside. Crime rates, traffic congestion and atmospheric pollution are all higher than in the rest of the continent, as are mortality rates from diseases, accidents, poisoning and violence. Sydney is also the most expensive city in Australia, with median house prices by far the highest in the country. Much harbourside property exceeds $A1 million and larger houses are sold for more than $A10 million. Sydneysiders display keen interest in real estate prices and there is constant prognostication on how each property is appreciating in value. Some forty to fifty closely printed pages of the *Sydney Morning Herald* each Saturday advertise property sales and analyse price movements, while suburban newspapers are mainly vehicles for property advertisements. The high real estate prices have boosted the exodus of retired people from Sydney, mostly towards coastal areas and warmer climates such as Queensland, where housing and life generally is cheaper. Meanwhile, there is a continuing and accelerating trend by the well-off middle-class professionals to relocate from their once preferred leafy outer suburbs to the inner city areas. Former working-class suburbs, such as Paddington, Glebe and Balmain, have been gentrified with renovated and extended cottages, boutique shops, art galleries, trendy cafés and restaurants. As rates and rents escalate, the poorer population groups are forced out towards the metropolitan periphery, often a long distance from their workplace.

Sydney is obsessed with food. The more affluent inner-city dwellers are always out breakfasting, brunching, lunching and dining or having coffee and cake in one of the innumerable cafés. The large influx of immigrants from all over the world has provided a choice of well over 100 national cuisines. Visitors to the Olympic Games will be able to eat their own national food, should they wish to do so. However, a much more interesting gastronomic experience is offered by modern Australian cuisine, which is unique. It combines elements of European tradition and Asian techniques with fresh, high-quality local produce. The visiting diner should not miss out on sampling some of the many excellent Australian wines. Sydney has come a long way from the days when the Australian staple dish was a hefty serving of steak with chips, accompanied by a few lettuce leaves.

Besides the hedonistic pursuits of eating, drinking, jogging, surfing and sunbathing, Sydney offers a wide choice of cultural activities. The visual arts range from Aboriginal cave paintings (Sydney has more rock art than any other city in the world) through pioneering Australian artists like Tom Roberts and Arthur Streeton, whose works can be found in several of Sydney's art galleries, to post-modernism. A cultural highlight for the visitor interested in the art scene is a visit to the studio in Surry Hills, an inner suburb, of the internationally celebrated 'enfant terrible' painter Brett Whiteley, who died in tragic circumstances in 1992. His paintings of Sydney Harbour and Lavender Bay are outstanding. Sydney's most commercially successful artist is Ken Done, whose simple, colourful works decorate everything from coasters to T-shirts. He has a gallery in the Rocks and many retail centres also stock his works. The Art Gallery of New South Wales in the Domain has a large, representative collection of Australian art and a plethora of private galleries have continuous exhibitions of established and budding artists.

In 1935, as a result of the Depression, Sydney was reduced to only two theatres. Now there are more than a score of major theatrical venues and a vibrant drama movement fostered in suburban halls by students and amateur companies. There are also a number of theatre restaurants.

The biggest impetus on the Sydney arts scene was the opening of the Sydney Opera House in 1973 on its prominent site on Bennelong Point jutting into the Harbour in the shadow of that other Sydney icon – the Harbour Bridge. Besides the Opera Theatre which seats 1,547, it contains the Concert hall with 2,679 seats, the Drama Theatre with 544 seats and the Playhouse with 398 seats. A wide range of performances is presented in these venues, including orchestral concerts, opera, dance, plays, chamber music, jazz, musicals, pop concerts and a host of other entertainment. The Opera House is Australia's most popular tourist attraction.

The month-long Sydney Festival in January is the culmination of the arts year and Sydneysiders take to it with gusto. The plays, concerts, performances, exhibitions and other events suit all tastes and budgets. Nearly fifty different venues ranging from the Opera House to the Bondi Beach Pavillion offer opera, outdoor films, art showings, street theatre, writers' festivals and jazz. The festival attracts buskers and other amateurs and performing enthusiasts line the city streets. Some of the most popular events take advantage of the balmy summer climate and enormous, free, open air concerts take place in the Domain, such as Opera in the Park and Symphony under the Stars with thousands of Sydneysiders picnicking on the Park's grassy expanses.

In 1993 Sydney was awarded the Year 2000 Olympic Games – it became the Olympic city. Much of the Olympic infrastructure was completed by late 1999. It centres on Homebush Bay, formerly a semi-abandoned industrial landscape, now transformed into a modern complex of sporting facilities, eateries and residential development. Stadium Australia, where the opening and closing ceremonies will take place, as well as the athletics events and the soccer final, has seating for 107,000 spectators and has already hosted several large sporting events. The Sydney International Aquatic Centre has been in operation for several years and the Sydney Super Dome, the largest indoor stadium in Australia with a capacity for 18,000, opened in October 1999. In September 2000 Sydney will have an influx of several million local and international spectators. To cope with the greatly increased demands on the public transport facilities, the system is being extensively improved, with new expressways and railway lines linking Sydney's Kingsford Smith Airport to the Olympic site.

As if to demonstrate that Sydney's greatest industry lies in hedonism, on 31 December 1999 the city organized a multi-million dollar extravaganza to mark the arrival of the new millennium. Over one million people crowded

Introduction

the Sydney Harbour foreshores to enjoy a range of free entertainment and a spectacular display of fireworks, which some international commentators watching the NCC world-wide television hook-up rated as the best in the world. The large turnout of Sydneysiders within the city area provided the organizers, at the cost of five million dollars of taxpayers' money, with a useful practice in crowd control in preparation for the seventeen days of the Olympic Games in September 2000.

Brassy and confident, Sydney looks forward to the new millennium as Australia's favourite metropolis.

About the bibliography

This bibliography directs the reader to books on all aspects of Sydney and its people. The selection emphasizes sources which explain those aspects of Sydney which, in the compiler's view, express its unique qualities and background. It is hoped that the works included will stimulate the reader's curiosity about Australia's largest and most cosmopolitan city and encourage further reading. It is important to remember that Australia's white settlement began in Sydney in 1788. Books dealing with early Australian and New South Wales colonial history have Sydney and its region as their focus, especially for the first forty or so years. Such works have been included in the bibliography.

The book is intended for the informed general reader, as well as for the scholar who wishes to obtain background information in a field other than his own. It should be useful to short- and long-term visitors and intending immigrants, or persons interested in transacting business in Sydney. It will serve as a reference tool for librarians, booksellers and others, who are frequently asked to recommend books in a particular subject area, and can be used as a selection tool by librarians wishing to assemble or develop collections on Sydney.

The selection of suitable titles for inclusion in the bibliography was done in the National Library of Australia in Canberra. Being a legal deposit institution for Australian publications, it holds all of the books included in the bibliography. All of the selections were examined by the compiler and book reviews were also used in exercising choice for inclusion.

The bibliography includes classic accounts, general surveys, thorough summaries and books which, for want of a better phrase, add 'local colour', and hopefully will kindle a spark of curiosity in the reader to delve deeper and further. Such a keen reader will note that many of the listed titles contain extensive bibliographies or suggestions for further reading. Following the truism that 'a picture is worth a thousand words', pictorial works and those generously illustrated have an honoured place in the bibliography.

The monograph literature about Sydney does not cover every aspect of the city and the life of its people adequately. Biographies, which throw light on the wider field of endeavour of the biographee, or which fill a gap in the literature in a particular field of knowledge, have been included within appropriate subject sections. Genealogical works have been excluded. Selected works of fiction and poetry, when they illuminate some important aspect of Sydney, are included. As far as possible, the arrangement of books within each section is hierarchical. The general introductions and surveys of the subject are followed by works of specialized interest and increasing complexity. The intended audience of a book is often indicated in the annotation.

Although the emphasis of the bibliography is on books, the more important newspapers, periodicals and magazines are listed. The National Library On-line Public Access Catalogue (OPAC) may be accessed via the Internet or via modem. A wide range of other resources are also available from the Library's World Wide Web (WWW) server. This site not only provides links to the catalogue, but also access to many indexes and guides, including periodical indexes for readers interested in journal and newspaper literature.

Throughout this bibliography the emphasis is on recent publications, some of which may be available from specialist bookshops in English-speaking countries, but those wishing to purchase may be more successful writing directly to the publishers. Older works, as well as more recent ones which are out of print, should be available on interlibrary loan from national or university libraries, especially those that have some involvement with Australian studies.

I am grateful for the assistance given to me by Maija Kepars who unselfishly acted the part of the informed general reader by critically commenting on the language, content and general comprehensibility of the annotations which describe each entry in the bibliography. Ms Kepars was also responsible for the onerous task of word processing the bibliography.

I. Kepars
January 2000

Sydney and Its People

General

1 Sydney.
Geoffrey Moorhouse. Sydney: Allen & Unwin, 1999. 277p. bibliog.

The noted British travel writer, author of *Calcutta* and *Imperial city: the rise and rise of New York*, here pays tribute to Sydney and its people. He has been quoted in the press: 'No other city was born under so cruel a star but no other city now gives the impressionable visitor such a feeling of still boundless optimism'. This statement underpins the book which is valuable for the outsider's view of Sydney.

2 Sydney.
Jan Morris. Melbourne: Penguin Books, 1993. 246p.

The noted English travel writer has produced a fascinating portrait of Australia's largest and most invigorating city. The book includes pictures and a map. It is a must for every potential visitor for the outsider's view of Sydney that it provides.

3 Ruth Park's Sydney.
Revised by Ruth Park, Rafe Champion. Sydney: Duffy & Snellgrove, 1999. rev. and expanded 2nd ed. 256p. maps.

This is a revised edition of the highly recommended guide to Sydney, published in 1973 in the *Companion Guide* series. It is a novelist's guide to Sydney, evocatively written in sparkling prose. Park, the author of best-selling novels and children's books, takes the reader to a city area, describes and explains it and then brings to life the men and women whose names are associated with the locality. Their personal history, foibles, scandals and good works are dissected and brought to life in relation to the physical environment. The nine chapters begin with maps outlining the walks. Well-selected photographs accompany the text. This is a book for reading before setting out, dipping into during the walk and rereading on returning home.

4 Sydney: the harbour city.

Paintings by Jeff Rigby, text by John Kingsmill. Sydney: Pierson in association with Macquarie Galleries Sydney, 1988. 159p.

In this large-format book, two Sydneysiders born and bred, a painter and a writer, have combined to create a loving portrait of Sydney. It is a must for visitors who wish to understand the city and its people.

5 Surface city: Sydney at the millennium.

Peter Murphy, Sophie Watson. Sydney: Pluto Press, 1997. 181p. maps. bibliogs.

An examination of the city, which will host the 2000 Olympic Games, from a number of aspects. Basing their work on recent social research, the authors analyse the selling of Sydney as a multiple destination; the 'multicultural' success story; economic restructuring since the 1970s and its impact on suburban lifestyles, social stratification and the ghettos; women's experiences of the city; and the problems of resource management for future development.

6 Sydney: people & places.

Margaret Throsby, Graham McCarter. Sydney: Australian Broadcasting Corporation, 1992. 119p.

This book reveals how fifty-four prominent Sydneysiders feel about their city. All are people who have attained eminence in their chosen fields of endeavour – the arts, academia, politics, public life, advertising and the law. The reader obtains an intimate view about the abstract aspects of Sydney: its energy, the casualness of its lifestyle and its attractive quality of life. Photographs of each contributor accompany the text and biographical notes are appended.

7 The 100 things everyone needs to know about Sydney.

David Dale, illustrations by Cathy Wilcox. Sydney: Pan Macmillan, 1997. 286p. bibliog.

Not a guidebook, but rather an informal listing of what Sydney eats, watches, fears, loves, gossips about, dances to and laughs at. In the author's words: 'This book is for people who want to form a relationship with Sydney, not just a one night stand'. The guide should be very useful for Sydneysiders and for those who want to become Sydneysiders, as well as for visitors wishing to get the flavour of a hedonist's paradise. David Dale has been a resident of Sydney for more than twenty years and has published widely on travel. He is the author of *The 100 things everyone needs to know about Australia* (Sydney: Pan Macmillan, 1996. 230p.).

8 The Sydney–Melbourne book.

Edited by Jim Davidson. Sydney: Allen & Unwin, 1986. 337p. bibliog.

The book presents a systematic comparison of Sydney and Melbourne – the pre-eminent cities in Australia where over forty per cent of the population resides. The emphasis is on cultural life with minimal consideration of the economic, developmental and historical aspects of the two cities.

9 Australian cultural elites: intellectual traditions in Sydney and Melbourne.
John Docker.   Sydney: Angus & Robertson, 1974. 182p. bibliog.

Melbourne and Sydney, the two largest cities in the country, have always been rivals on the popular plane. Docker extends the rivalry to the differing intellectual traditions of each city and demonstrates how these have produced contrary concerns among their intellectuals: a different style of politics and differing forms of artistic expression.

10 Seven cities of Australia.
Sydney: John Ferguson, 1978. 182p.

In 1977 the *Bulletin* magazine asked seven noted Australian writers to take an extended look at the capital city with which each was connected in some way. Ian Moffitt made an affectionate assessment of Sydney; Hal Porter gave a brilliant portrait of the smallest capital, Hobart; Robert Macklin wrote about Brisbane; Keith Dunstan, a Melbourne newspaper columnist, took a close look at his native city; Geoffrey Dutton, a noted literary figure, examined Adelaide; Robert Drewe made an expatriate's return to remote Perth in Western Australia; and Alan Fitzgerald, Canberra's resident satirist, wrote about the nation's capital. The articles have been collected as a permanent record of Australia's capital cities in the late 1970s. Black-and-white illustrations accompany the text.

11 Sydney.
Text by Gavin Souter, photographs by Quinton Davis.   Sydney: Angus & Robertson, 1965. 84p.

Gavin Souter, a noted journalist, author of several well-received books and life-long Sydneysider, presents a hymn to the city he loves. In impressionistic, stylish prose, complemented by Quinton Davis' photographs, he evokes the geography, buildings, smells, atmosphere and people of the city, which, in the author's words, since the 1950s, 'became more concerned about intellectual issues, less self-conscious about the arts, more permissive in its social attitudes and less considerate of sacred cows'. In short, Sydney became the modern city as everyone knows it today.

12 Saga of Sydney: the birth, growth and maturity of the mother city of Australia.
Frank Clune.   Sydney: Halstead Press, 1961. 508p.

This is an exploration of Sydney by the historical popularizer Frank Clune, author of over a hundred books on travel, history and biography. It gives a view of Sydney at the end of the 1950s, when the foundations for the Sydney Opera House were laid. A feature of the book is its emphasis on the history of leading commercial and industrial firms. There are also 113 illustrations and 17 maps.

13 My town: Sydney in the 1930s.
Lydia Gill.   Sydney: State Library of New South Wales Press, 1993. 161p.

The author was born in Sydney in 1913 and has lived there for most of her life. She grew up during the Depression and Second World War and it was during this period that she developed her intimate and comprehensive knowledge of the Sydney scene. In this book of reminiscences she brings Sydney to life during the 1930s in a mixture of nostalgia, commentary and social history. The text is supplemented with many contemporary photographs.

14   The naked city.
    The Sun-Herald.   Sydney: The Sun-Herald, 1992. 168p.

Selected from the popular column, 'The Naked City', which first appeared in the Sydney tabloid *The Sun-Herald* in March 1990, these articles present a journalistic kaleidoscope of Sydney events and personalities, ranging from the high life to the low life.

Pictorial works

15   Above Sydney: aerial views of the world's most beautiful city.
    George Hall.   Sydney: Lansdowne, 1999. 2nd ed. 200p.

This sumptuous, large-format book, packed with spectacular aerial photographs in colour, depicts Sydney from the air. First published in 1984, this is an up-to-date panorama of the Olympic city by one of the world's foremost aerial photographers, George Hall.

16   Quintessential Sydney.
    Edited by Gerry North.   Sydney: Tower Books, 1999. 159p.

A collection by photographers with a passion for Sydney, portraying the 'real' Sydneysiders – non-glamorous, 'ordinary' inhabitants going about their everyday business: fishing, playing bingo, shopping, swimming, worshipping and misbehaving.

17   Sydney.
    Wildlight Photo Agency.   Sydney: Hardie Grant Books, 1998. 116p.

An up-to-date panorama of Sydney consisting of colour photographs of the city and the activities of its citizens by members of the Wildlight Photo Agency. It is designed for the armchair traveller or visitor.

18   Sydney: city of sails.
    Photographers: Shaen Adey, Nick Rains, Anthony Johnson.   Sydney: New Holland, 1998. 128p.

This large-format book is a visual celebration of metropolitan Sydney with over 130 full-colour photographs and panoramas that attempt to capture the essence of the city and its region.

19   Sydney 2000: the Olympic city.
    Ken Duncan.   Sydney: Ken Duncan Photographs, 1998. 80p.

Award-winning photographer Ken Duncan provides a glimpse into the heart and soul of Sydney with this collection of colour images. They are his tribute to Australia's Olympic city. Visitors to the Games in the year 2000 can acquaint themselves with Sydney in its unique natural setting prior to their arrival through this collection of colour photographs.

20   This is Sydney.
Text by Wendy Moore.   Sydney: New Holland, 1996. 160p.

A large-format book which describes Sydney in words and pictures. Approximately one-third of the book is devoted to text, describing history and contemporary city highlights, such as the Rocks area in the shadow of the Harbour Bridge, the Harbour and its ferries, national parks, the modern icons – Sydney Harbour Bridge and the Opera House – the varied architecture and the magnificent beaches, as well as Sydney's picturesque surroundings. The rest of the book is taken up by colour photographs of Sydney and its inhabitants engaged in recreational pursuits.

21   Sydneyside.
Richard Whitaker.   Sydney: Gregory's, 1986. 214p. maps. bibliog.

A history of Sydney's development through the use of past and present photographs, old maps, engravings and advertisements. The author has scoured extensively through guide-books and street directories to find 'then and now' photographs from exact locations in the city. This large and lavishly illustrated book is a most interesting aid to learn about Sydney's evolution over the past 150 years.

22   Sydney's beaches: from Palm Beach to Cronulla.
Warwick Kent.   Sydney: New Holland, 1998. 112p. map.

Sydney has more than thirty ocean beaches, stretching from Palm Beach in the north to Cronulla in the south. Seventy kilometres of beautiful coastline offers a variety of conditions for the surfer, the fisherman and the family. The book consists of panoramic colour photographs and a large map which indicates the location of each beach.

23   Cats of Sydney.
Paul Burrows.   Sydney: Random House, 1997. unpaginated.

This large-format book contains some 200 artistic photographs of cats in various parts of Sydney, taken by a cat-loving professional photographer. While concentrating on the animals, the photographs also include as background unusual shots of the city and its suburbs.

24   The Sydney we love.
Ruth Park, Cedric Emanuel.   Melbourne: Nelson, 1987. 134p.

Written by long-time resident of Sydney and renowned author Ruth Park and illustrated by Cedric Emanuel, one of Australia's most popular landscape artists, this large-format book is immensely readable and is an elegant pictorial record of Sydney. It is recommended to the first-time visitor to the city.

25   Sprod's views of Sydney.
George Sprod.   Sydney: Kangaroo Press, 1981. 88p.

'It's the oldest, the largest, the most historic and in the eyes of its inhabitants (some of whom have been as far as Cootamundra) the greatest in the world' – this is how artist and writer George Sprod describes his adopted city of Sydney in words, drawings and cartoons in a short, but delightful book. It is a humorous introduction to the city and its citizens. He has also written a light-hearted autobiography *Life on a square-wheeled bike,* published in 1984.

26 Life at the Cross.
Text by Kenneth Slessor, photographs by Robert Walker. Adelaide: Rigby, 1965. 120p.

A photographic essay about life in Kings Cross during its heyday as the Bohemian headquarters of Sydney. Today the area has deteriorated into a row of strip-joints and sleazy bars. The 200 evocative photographs of the past are linked by text provided by Kenneth Slessor, poet and journalist and a denizen of the Cross for many years.

27 Waterways of Sydney: a sketchbook.
Drawings by Cedric Emanuel, text by Geoffrey Dutton. Melbourne: Dent, 1988. 55p.

What makes Sydney unique is the omnipresence of water. The city is permeated by water – the magnificent harbour, the ocean, the rivers and the creeks. This book takes the reader on a guided tour of this vast and fascinating water world. With magnificent drawings by celebrated landscape artist Cedric Emanuel and the descriptive text of Geoffrey Dutton, this book is eminently suitable for browsing.

28 Historic Sydney as seen by its early artists.
Susanna de Vries-Evans. Sydney: Angus & Robertson, 1987. rev. ed. 160p. bibliog.

This large-format book contains 120 paintings, drawings and sketches by a variety of professional and amateur artists, who depict the growth of Sydney in its first 100 years, 1788-1888. The illustrations are accompanied by detailed descriptions of the subject of each picture and the artist responsible for it.

29 Sydney illustrated (1842-3).
J. Skinner Prout, with letterpress description by John Rae. Sydney: Tyrrell's, 1949. 102p.

The book consists of fourteen plates in full colour by John Skinner Prout, who painted the originals in the year in which Sydney became a corporation, 1842-43, with letterpress by John Rae, the first town clerk of Sydney. The paintings and the text provide a faithful description of the Sydney of the 1840s.

30 Victorian and Edwardian Sydney from old photographs.
Selected and introduced by Eric Russell, designed by Quinton F. Davis. Sydney: John Ferguson, 1975. unpaginated.

Presents a selection of 200 old photographs spanning the reigns of Queen Victoria and King Edward VII from the mid-1850s to the period just prior to the outbreak of the First World War. It presents Sydney and its inhabitants in eight sections: The city; Out in the suburbs; Emporiums and shops; Disasters, events and occasions; Sydneysiders at work; Theatres, hotels, pubs; Public transport; and A few Sydneysiders. Overall, the book offers a fascinating insight into the Sydney of that era and proves the old adage, that a picture is worth a thousand words.

31 Phillip Geeves presents Cazneaux's Sydney 1904-1934.
Phillip Geeves, photograph selection and biography by Gael Newton.
Sydney: David Ell Press, 1980. 144p.

Harold Cazneaux's long and distinguished career as one of Australia's foremost photographers stretched from 1904 when he first began taking photographs, until his death in 1953. He is best remembered for his pictures of Sydney where he lived from 1904 onwards. In this book there are reproductions of many of his best photographs which present a picture of Sydney and its people in the early part of this century. Popular historian Phillip Geeves has written the historical text which accompanies each photograph. Lovers of photography as well as general readers will enjoy this collection.

32 Phillip Geeves' Sydney.
Phillip Geeves, drawings by Cedric Emanuel. Sydney: Angus & Robertson, 1981. 157p.

A book of sketches of historical buildings of Sydney by noted artist Cedric Emanuel, with descriptive notes by Sydney's popular historian Phillip Geeves. This is a delightful volume for browsing.

Guidebooks

General

33 2000 things to see and do in Sydney: your guide to the best of Sydney's attractions.
Edited by Lee Atkinson, text by Jillian McFarlane and others.
Sydney: NRMA Publications, 1999. 136p. maps.

This is the insider's guide to the Olympic city. There are detailed guides to beaches, swimming pools, shops, restaurants, pubs, parks, entertainment, museums, Aboriginal sites, tours, sport, transport, wildlife and events. Costs, opening hours and telephone numbers to venues are given and clear maps show their location. An attractive publication with many colour photographs, it has been produced by the staff of *The Open Road,* the official magazine of NRMA Ltd, the New South Wales motorists' association.

34 Seven days in Sydney: the guide to Sydney Australia.
David Messent, Graham White.   Sydney: David Messent Photography, 1998. rev. ed. 176p. maps.

Intended for the short-term visitor, this book describes seven tours of the harbour city, all starting and finishing at Circular Quay, the city's main ferry terminal. The book is lavishly illustrated with colour photographs and detailed maps are provided. A similar book by Messent is *Sydney's birthplace: the Rocks.*

35 Sydney in a week.
Wendy Moore.   Sydney: New Holland, 1997. 176p. maps.

This guide to Sydney includes seven comprehensive day tours and eight special itineraries, including tours to the Hunter Valley vineyards and the southern and northern beaches. Transport options are given and there are useful directories for easily reached restaurants, shops and nightspots. The highlight of the book is the 240 spectacular photographs, including aerial photographs with captions of main features. There are also seventeen detailed maps.

36   Sydney & surrounds.
Text by Jan Bowen.   Sydney: Random House, 1998. 285p. maps.
(Discover Australia Series).

A conveniently sized guidebook packed with information and maps for enjoying one of the world's top tourist destinations. It covers Sydney's landmarks, heritage and natural environment, sightseeing, shopping, arts and entertainment, museums and galleries, restaurants and cafés, beaches and bushwalks, sports and open air activities and suggests various destinations. One of the features of the book is that it takes the visitor beyond the Harbour Bridge and Opera House into the surrounding countryside which can be spectacular. Also covered are the Central Coast, Hunter Valley vineyards, Canberra, the Southern Highlands, Blue Mountains and South Coast as well as nearby national parks. Colour illustrations are scattered throughout the book.

37   Sydney: a Lonely Planet city guide.
Tom Smallman.   Melbourne: Lonely Planet, 1997. 3rd ed. 294p.
maps.

This is the third edition of Lonely Planet's comprehensive guide to Sydney. Lonely Planet guides to most parts of the world have achieved recognition as leaders in the field and this guide continues to uphold the standard with all the usual features: colour maps, accommodation and restaurant listings, information on how to get around the city and suburbs, shopping, surfing and excursions to the Blue Mountains, Hawkesbury River and the Hunter Valley vineyards. Published in a handy pocket-size, it is recommended to all visitors to Sydney.

38   Time out Sydney guide.
Melbourne: Penguin Books, 1997. 290p. maps. bibliog.

Well written by a team of journalists, this publication contains all the general features of guidebooks. It is the first edition to be issued in a convenient size. It aims to publish updates and one is expected before the 2000 Olympic Games. Penguin Books has also been granted exclusive licence to market a whole series of practical Olympics-related publications, from maps and guides to book packs for children. These will be published from March 2000 onward in the run-up to the September 2000 opening of the Olympic Games.

39   Sydney.
Main contributors Ken Brass, Kirsty McKenzie.   London: Dorling
Kindersley, 1996. 264p. maps. tables. (Eyewitness Travel Guides).

Published in the widely available Dorling Kindersley Eyewitness Travel Guides series, which covers many countries and cities of the world, this has all the well-known visual features of the other guides in the series. There are more than 600 full-colour photographs of Sydney and surrounding area, detailed maps of all parts of the city, cross-sections and floorplans of public buildings and landmarks, and detailed information on each sight. In addition, there are wide-ranging listings of Sydney's best shops, pubs, beaches, entertainment venues, hotels, restaurants and cafés in all price ranges. This guide should be studied and carried before and during a visit to the harbour city.

40 Free and low-cost Sydney.
Jenny Crocker, Julia Collingwood.   Sydney: Choice Books, 1999.
136p.

Written for residents of Sydney, or visitors who wish to enjoy entirely free or low-cost
activities in Sydney and its suburbs. The guide lists a bewildering range of things to do
or visit and has been compiled by the Australian Consumer's Association, an
independent, non-profit organization dedicated to working on behalf of Australian
consumers.

41 This Week in Sydney.
Sydney: APN News & Media, 1997- . monthly.

A regular guide to coming events and tourist attractions in Sydney. It contains detailed
maps of the city, ferry services and the CityRail suburban network. It is available free to
visitors and tourists at points of arrival and at Visitor Information Centres.

42 Sydney Visitors Guide.
Sydney: Pacific Access on behalf of Telstra Corporation, 1997- .
quarterly.

This is a free guide (paid by advertisers) containing useful information to help visitors
find their way around Sydney. Features include: detailed maps, a what's on guide,
attractions, public transport information, shopping areas, entertainment guide and a
telephone directory section. The guide has been produced with the assistance of Tourism
New South Wales and is available at major tourism outlets and Visitor Information
Centres in New South Wales, including the Sydney Visitors Centre, 106 George Street,
The Rocks.

**43 The Sydney Morning Herald best of Sydney: the A–Z guide to the
Olympic city.**
Edited by Ross Muller.   Sydney: SMH Books, 1998. 356p. maps.

This guidebook is written by the people who know Sydney best, more than eighty of the
Sydney Morning Herald's leading news, sports, arts and lifestyle journalists. The book
contains A-Z listings for more than 280 categories: arts and entertainment, food and
drink, fashion and beauty, sport and outdoor activities, home shopping and services,
sightseeing and tourist facilities. There is a locality guide to more than 1,500 shops,
venues, businesses and facilities, as well as a calendar of Sydney events for 1999 and a
complete practical guide for visitors. It is a handy companion volume to the telephone
book and the street directory.

**44 Gregory's 200 kilometres around Sydney: your essential guide to
Sydney and surrounds.**
Sydney: Gregory's, 1999. 37th ed. 287p. maps.

Published since 1934, this is the most comprehensive guide to the Sydney region for
locals and tourists alike. The guide contains suggested tours, a list of 'must see', 'must
do' attractions, natural features, history, hints on getting there and getting around,
festivals and events, national parks, parks and gardens and recreational activities. There
are detailed new regional and locality maps as well as suggested walking maps. In

addition, there are over 450 colour photographs. This attractive book is an essential glove box companion to *Gregory's Sydney 1999 compact street directory* (see item no. 47).

45 Day trips around Sydney: a daytrippers guide to 200 km around Sydney.
Bruce Elder.   Melbourne: Lothian, 1993. 128p. maps.

The Sydney region contains a wonderful diversity of natural attractions. Beaches, national parks, mountains, historic towns and rural and seaside retreats abound. This book provides information on twenty-five trips to the most interesting destinations, with detailed descriptions of highlights on the journey. The maps are hand-drawn and it will be necessary for visitors to carry a proper road map with them on the tours.

46 Picture of Sydney and stranger's guide in New South Wales for 1839.
James Maclehose.   Sydney: John Ferguson in association with The Royal Australian Historical Society, 1977. 186p. map.

An excellent early guide to Sydney, first published in 1839. The book contains practical information for the visitor or intending immigrant and is illustrated with forty-four engravings of public buildings, land and water views around Sydney. The book begins with an 'historial memorandum of New South Wales, its government and its governors'. Then follows a description of Sydney's streets, public buildings, churches, places of education, amusements and detention. It concludes with a summary of the geography of the colony and a list of merchants, agents and brokers and their places of work.

Specific features

47 Gregory's Sydney 1999 compact street directory.
Sydney: Gregory's Publishing, 1999. 16th ed. 722p.

The latest edition of this indispensable street directory covers all of the Sydney metropolitan area and also contains a fully revised and updated Sydney city guide. This guide gives information on where to go and what to do in the city area. It covers sights, shopping and markets, culture and entertainment, restaurants and cafés, bars, clubs and pubs. For people who want to venture outside Sydney, there is the *UBD City link 1999 street directory*, which as well as the Sydney street directory, also includes the Blue Mountains, Canberra, Central Coast, Newcastle and Wollongong.

48 Walking Sydney.
Lisa Clifford, Mandy Webb.   Sydney: Pan Macmillan, 1997. 213p. maps.

This guide details twenty-five of the city's best walks, from gentle strolls in the Botanic Gardens to day-long hikes through unspoilt national park bushland. It includes cliff-top paths with ocean and city views, beaches, historic sights and Aboriginal rock carvings, museums, galleries and shops. Each walk is accompanied by an easy-to-follow map, together with key facts on the walk itself, such as duration of the walk, facilities and how to get to and from the starting point. There are detailed descriptions of points of interest along the way and information on the history and background of many of Sydney's most interesting sights. The guide caters for walkers of all ages and all interests.

49 Sydney good walks guide.
Joan Lawrence.   Sydney: Kingsclear Books, 1999. 2nd ed. 230p. maps. bibliog.

This book contains details of 180 walks, each with a map and covering every municipality of Sydney. Each walk includes information about distance, pace, access by public transport and the features of the walk, which include the history of the area, bushland and beauty spots, architecture, waterways, flora and fauna. The author has written over a dozen books on Sydney history and has conducted historic walks around Sydney for twelve years.

50 Sydney strolls: eastern suburbs.
Graham Spindler.   Sydney: New Holland, 1999. 96p. maps.

The best way to acquaint yourself with a strange place is to walk around it. This booklet contains details of thirteen walks in Sydney's most affluent area, the eastern suburbs, stretching from the city along the southern shores of the Harbour to the ocean. There are clearly drawn route maps which are cross-referenced to the text and the usual features of walking guides, such as the highlights, length, duration and degree of difficulty of each walk, access to facilities and street directory references. Each walk also features a special-interest box, which range from bohemia and murder mysteries to policing beach culture. A second book in the series by Spindler features fourteen walks along the suburbs on Sydney Harbour's northern shores: *Sydney strolls: lower North Shore,* also published in 1999.

51 Best Sydney bushwalks.
Neil Paton.   Sydney: Kangaroo Press, 1998. 176p. maps.

One of the greatest features of Sydney as a city, is its proximity to large areas of natural bushland – few large cities in the world are blessed with so much wilderness around them. This guide includes details of sixty walks, which the author, an experienced walker, believes are the choicest available within the Sydney metropolitan area. The text is accompanied by clear maps and gives guidance on time and grade of difficulty for each walk. Photographs taken on these walks are proof that it is possible to get away from it all without leaving Sydney. A similar publication, listing thirty walks, is Alan Fairley's *Sydney's best bushland walks* (Sydney: Envirobook, 1993. 168p.). In 1997 and 1998 the National Parks Association of New South Wales published two volumes of *Bushwalks in the Sydney region* by S. Lord and G. Daniel. These include the National Parks of the Sydney region where some of the walks described take up to three days to complete.

52 The Sydney beach guide: plus the Central Coast.
David Crowe.   Melbourne: Mandarin, 1996. 206p. maps. bibliog.

Sydney is blessed with beautiful beaches and a climate which allows all year-round surfing enjoyment to thousands of Sydneysiders. This is the ultimate guide to 125 beaches within the metropolitan area and the nearby northern region. Key facts are provided for each beach with a little background information on its history. Information about safety aspects, especially important for ocean beaches, beach patrols, past and present pollution levels and facilities, such as shops, public transport and accessibility by car (for which road maps are provided), bushwalking, cycling, sailboarding, attractions for children and other amusements available in the vicinity is included. This is an indispensable guide to all swimmers, surfers and other visitors keen to sample a popular Australian pastime.

53 Guide to parks of Sydney.
Paul Knox, photographs by John Callanan. Sydney: UNSW Press, 1996. 160p. maps.

This guidebook presents a listing of a selection of the best public parks in and around Sydney. Each entry includes information on how to get to the park, its attractions, hours of opening and facilities provided. Information on public transport is also included. The author is a landscape architect with an intimate knowledge of many of the parks in his professional capacity. The book is profusely illustrated with colour photographs. There are sketch maps of the layout of the larger parks.

54 The wishing tree: a guide to memorial trees, statues, fountains, etc. in the Royal Botanic Gardens, Domain and Centennial Park, Sydney.
Edwin Wilson. Sydney: Kangaroo Press in association with the Royal Botanic Gardens, 1992. 160p. bibliog.

Sydney's Royal Botanic Gardens and the Domain, situated as they are between the Central Business District and the harbour, act as the city's lungs and are a favourite destination for Sydneysiders and tourists alike. Centennial Park, a few kilometres away, is a popular recreation area. The author of this guide provides a detailed study and catalogue of the numerous statues, fountains, gates, buildings and memorial trees to add to the enjoyment of visitors to these public spaces. Many of the commentaries are accompanied by illustrations.

55 Accessing Sydney: a handbook for people with disabilities and those who have problems getting around.
Edited by Charlotte Smedley. Sydney: ACROD N.S.W., 1994. 298p. bibliog.

This guide has been researched and written by a team of occupational therapists and people with disabilities, using the Australian Standard AS 1428.1 (1993). Information about the physical access to a wide variety of venues will assist visitors and travellers in finding their way around Sydney and its attractions. This book is intended to be used in conjunction with general tourist guides, as it does not duplicate general tourist information available in the standard guides. With the Paralympics scheduled for the year 2000, a second edition may be published to update this 1994 guidebook.

56 Picture Sydney: the traveller's photo guide.
Written and photographed by Tony Martorano. Sydney: DHQ Publishing, 1997. 128p. maps.

Published in a convenient pocket-sized edition and written by a professional photographer, this booklet shows the visitor to Sydney how to take the best photographs of the city's main attractions. Easy-to-read maps guide the visitor to the attractions and

Guidebooks. Specific features

there is a very useful service guide to film suppliers, developers, camera repairs and other handy tips. This guide is quite indispensable for the camera buff as well as the amateur who wants to take holiday snapshots.

Sydney Harbour

57 The complete guide to Sydney Harbour.
David Messent, David McGonigal.   Sydney: David Messent
Photography, 1994. 160p.

A pictorial work of colour aerial photographs with linking text depicting the magnificent Sydney Harbour. A section of detailed street maps of the foreshore and surrounding areas is appended to the volume. Other, earlier volumes concerning the Harbour and human activities on and around it are: *Port Jackson 200,* by Graeme Andrews (Frenchs Forest, New South Wales: Reed, 1986. 173p.); *A history of picturesque Sydney Harbour,* by Robyn Howard (Sydney: View Productions, 1984. 125p.); and *Sydney Harbour: a pictorial history from the first settlers to the present day,* by Michael Stringer (Narrabeen, New South Wales: J.M.A. Stringer & Co., 1984. 240p.).

58 Sydney Harbour.
David Moore, text by Rodney Hall.   Sydney: Chapter & Verse in
association with State Library of NSW Press, 1993. 184p.

In this large volume master photographer David Moore reveals his lifelong fascination with Sydney Harbour. With a final selection of over 200 images from many thousands, he has assembled a rich collection of photographs, both in colour and in black-and-white, spanning half a century. The images record the many moods and activities of one of the world's finest waterways as well as the developing city on its foreshores. The pictures are enriched by text by acclaimed novelist and poet Rodney Hall, who describes the city, its people and the harbour environment.

59 The history and description of Sydney Harbour.
P. R. Stephensen, Brian Kennedy.   Sydney: Reed, 1980. 352p.

This is an update by Brian Kennedy of the original work by Stephensen published in 1966. Often referred to as the world's greatest and most beautiful waterway, this great expanse of water, which meanders through the city and its outlying suburbs, not only serves the purpose of a haven for ships, but also acts as a water playground for Sydney's nearly four million citizens.

60   The waterways of Sydney Harbour.
Phillip Mathews.   Sydney: Phillip Mathews Book Publishers, 1997. 104p. maps.

A book for the boating enthusiast who wants to navigate the many waterways of Sydney Harbour. Every bay, promontory and tiny cave in its 240 kilometres of foreshore is described. Maps show soundings to the nearest half-metre, as well as main roads connecting with the shoreline. The book is richly illustrated with colour photographs taken from unique angles.

61   Waterfront Sydney: 1860-1920.
Graeme Aplin, John Storey.   Sydney: Allen & Unwin, 1991. 144p.

A collection of rare black-and-white photographs spanning the years 1860 to 1920 to illustrate the history of one of the world's great harbours. The authors provide a foreword discussing the role of the harbour in the life of Sydney. Each section of the book includes a map of the harbour with a key to the location of the place from which each photograph was taken.

62   A tribute to Sydney.
Lloyd Rees.   Sydney: The Macquarie Galleries, 1979. 63p.

As the noted landscape artist states in the preface, the series of paintings reproduced in this book is the result of his love affair with Sydney's wonderful harbour since he first saw it in 1916.

63   From the Quay.
Harvey Shore.   Sydney: NSWU Press, 1981. 192p. maps. bibliog.

For seventy years the various administrative bodies which controlled Sydney Harbour collected thousands of glass photographic plates. The last of these bodies recording the major changes in Sydney's and the Harbour's history was the Sydney Harbour Trust (1901-36). The collected plates remained forgotten until the author's investigations led to their re-discovery in a locked room at the Maritime Services Board of New South Wales. The current publication is the first printed record of this unique major historical collection, showing the development of Australia's foremost city and its port.

64   The islands of Sydney Harbour.
Simon Davies.   Sydney: Hale & Iremonger, 1984. 88p. maps. bibliog.

Sydney Harbour – or by its formal name Port Jackson – had thirteen islands at the time of the arrival of the First Fleet in 1788. Due to human intervention, only eight distinct islands remain today. This large-format, illustrated book traces the history of the remaining eight islands and provides information on how they may be visited.

65   The Garden Island.
T. R. Frame.   Sydney: Kangaroo Press, 1990. 240p. maps. bibliog. plans.

Garden Island in Sydney Harbour has been the focus of all naval activity in Australia for over two centuries and has been the historic home of the Royal Australian Navy since its establishment in 1911. This is the first detailed history of this naval establishment. The island near the Central Business District of Sydney has long featured in the city's history as a place for the confinement of convicts, an Aboriginal burial ground, the site of Australia's first zoo and the base for naval operations during the Maori Wars, the Boxer Rebellion in China, the two World Wars, the Korean war and the war in Vietnam. The book will be useful to anyone with an interest in the Navy, ships, dockyards and the city of Sydney.

66 Sydney Harbour of yesteryear: the glass plate photography of William James Hall.

Jeff Toghill.   Sydney: Reed, 1982. 127p.

William James Hall was a photographer who recorded the yachting scene and the associated lifestyle of Sydney Harbour around the turn of the century. This book presents a large selection of those photographs, illustrating the ships, boats and the recreational life of Sydneysiders on the foreshores and in the waters of their magnificent Harbour.

Biographies, Autobiographies, Memoirs, Letters and Diaries

67   Sandstone gothic.
   Andrew Riemer.   Sydney: Allen & Unwin, 1998. 225p.

This is a pessimistic memoir of almost forty years spent by the author at the University of Sydney. After studying for an Arts degree at the University from 1956 to 1959, Riemer went to University College, London for postgraduate studies and returned to take up a career as an English literature academic at Sydney University in 1963. He retired from the University in 1994, because of disillusionment with faculty politics and academic life in general. The book examines his academic career in intimate detail and gives an insider's view of university life at Sydney over forty years. Upon retirement Riemer became a book reviewer and literary journalist. Sadly, there is no index.

68   Penny dreadful.
   Penelope Nelson.   Sydney: Random House, 1995. 247p.

This is a lively, nostalgic account of growing up in Sydney during the 1950s and 1960s. Penelope Nelson, a novelist and author, reminiscences about her youth in the affluent eastern suburbs of Sydney. She recounts her experiences at an exclusive girl's school, Frensham, and at Sydney University, where she worked on *Honi Soit,* the University's newspaper. Enlivened by wit and ironic reflection, the book is an excellent picture of life in Sydney in the post-war period as enjoyed by the privileged classes of society.

69   Manly girls.
   Elisabeth Wynhausen.   Melbourne: Penguin Books, 1989. 179p.

Wynhausen was born in Holland in 1936 and together with her Jewish family arrived in Sydney as a migrant in 1951. She was educated at Manly Girls High School and Sydney University. After teaching for a time at a boarding school for girls, she became a journalist working at several Sydney newspapers and magazines. This is a light-hearted look at growing up in and adjusting to Australian society in the Sydney of the 1960s and 1970s.

70 A kingdom by the sea.
Nancy Phelan.   Sydney: Angus & Robertson, 1990. 170p.

A new edition of the noted author's classic autobiography originally published in 1969. It is about growing up in Sydney's North Shore before the Great Depression. Humorously and stylishly written, the book evokes a way of life and a Sydney long since gone. It is a great read about suburban life in the innocent 1920s. In 1998 the University of Queensland Press published *Kingdom by the sea* with *Hearts of oak* in an omnibus edition. *Hearts of oak* is in a sense a sequel to Phelan's earlier books and tells of her subsequent experiences in England.

71 Homebush boy.
Tom Keneally.   Melbourne: Heinemann, 1995. 180p.

Today Keneally is the successful Booker Prize winner, the author of over twenty novels and some works of non-fiction. In this book he portrays himself as a sixteen-year-old Catholic boy in 1952, growing up in the Sydney western suburb of Homebush, the home of the 2000 Olympic Games. Well written in a humorous vein, the story gives a vivid picture of life of one year, one school and one suburb with a colourful cast of schoolboys, parents, siblings and neighbours.

72 An interrupted life.
Donald Horne.   Sydney: HarperCollins, 1998. 812p.

Horne is one of Australia's foremost social and cultural critics, journalist, academic and author of many acclaimed books. Probably his greatest literary achievement is his autobiography. The present book contains all three volumes: *The education of young Donald,* about his childhood and education in Sydney's western suburbs and later at Sydney University; *Confessions of a new boy*; and *Portrait of an optimist,* which continues the story to 1958 and relates his experiences as a journalist in Sydney. Overall, the autobiography chronicles life in Sydney in the 1930s, 1940s and 1950s, and achieves the distinction of being an important social document of the period. Sadly, this voluminous book lacks an index.

73 The boy Adeodatus: the portrait of a lucky young bastard.
Bernard Smith.   Melbourne: Oxford University Press, 1990. 301p.

This is the paperback edition of Bernard Smith's celebrated, award-winning autobiography, first published in 1984. Smith is one of Australia's pre-eminent historians and art critics. This book evokes his boyhood, growing up in the Sydney suburb of Burwood around the First World War. It continues through the 1920s and 1930s, following the changing values of his youth, and shows what it was like to be an emerging artist, socialist and intellectual in pre-war Sydney. The account stops in 1940 when he decided against becoming an artist and instead became involved with art as an academic.

74 The Queen of Bohemia: the autobiography of Dulcie Deamer.
Being *The golden decade* edited with an introduction by Peter Kirkpatrick.   Brisbane: University of Queensland Press, 1998. 239p. bibliog.

Dulcie Deamer (1890-1972) was a writer and journalist, and an irrepressible free spirit. Although her novels, poetry and plays have been largely forgotten, the Bohemian life in which she revelled during the 'golden decade' of the 1920s and up to the late 1960s, still stirs memories. Deamer was a freelance writer in King's Cross, a Bohemian refuge near the centre of Sydney, for fifty years. In 1925 she was crowned 'Queen of Bohemia' and two years later in another mock coronation, she became 'Empress of the Holy Bohemian Empire'. The book is not standard autobiography, but rather an impressionistic account of the glory days of Sydney's Bohemia – an evocation of an age.

75   Australia Street: a boy's-eye view of the 1920s and 1930s.
John Kingsmill.   Sydney: Hale & Iremonger, 1991. 192p.

Born in 1920 in Sydney, the author grew up during the 1920s and 1930s in a working-class family in the beachside suburb of Bondi. This is a social document providing glimpses of suburban values in a pre-Second World War, socially homogeneous Sydney. In 1990 Kingsmill published a more personal memoir entitled *The innocent: growing up in Bondi in the 1920s and 1930s* (North Ryde, New South Wales: Angus & Robertson, 1990. 222p.). Both books are excellent descriptions of the innocence of old Sydney and its inhabitants.

76   Children of one family: the story of Anthony and Ann Hordern and their descendants in Australia 1825-1925.
Lesley Hordern.   Sydney: Retford Press, 1985. 368p. bibliog.

The Hordern family have been prominent in commercial, pastoral and sporting circles in Sydney since the 1830s. This large book follows the Horderns' fortunes during their first century, tracing their story from the establishment of the first small shop to the building in Sydney of one of the largest emporiums in the world. Basing his work on extensive family records and other sources, the author, a Hordern by marriage, has produced a fascinating book with many illustrations. Besides the story of the growth of the retail trade in Sydney, perhaps unwittingly, the book gives an authentic insight into the life and activities of the moneyed classes of Sydney during the period 1825-1925.

77   Aunts up the Cross.
Robin Dalton.   Melbourne: Heinemann, 1997. new ed. 172p.

This memoir of growing up in Sydney's Kings Cross during the 1920s and 1930s, an area sometimes described as an antipodean Montmartre, was first published in 1965, and reprinted in 1980 and has become a minor classic. Dalton, a literary agent in London and lately a successful film producer, *Oscar and Lucinda* being her latest, chronicles life in a large house full of eccentrics in a colourful area, which in the author's words, 'doesn't attract writers, it creates them'. Witty and economical, the book evokes life in an era long past. After the Second World War the Cross gradually turned into a seedy area of strip clubs, prostitution and drug pushing.

78   Old books, old friends, old Sydney: the fascinating reminiscences of a Sydney bookseller.
James R. Tyrrell.   Sydney: Angus & Robertson, 1987. 219p.

James Tyrrell (1875-1961) was born in Sydney where in 1888 he joined the bookselling firm of Angus and Robertson. Here he moved from errand boy to manager, before leaving to set up his own shop in 1905. In 1914 he moved into publishing and also founded his famous second-hand bookshop, which became a meeting place for Sydney writers and literary figures. This book of memoirs, first published in 1952, which includes his boyhood reminiscences of Sydney and his recollections of the personalities of the book world, is an invaluable record of Sydney's social and cultural scene around the turn of the century. There are also 300 well-chosen illustrations, photographs of people and places, caricatures and cartoons and facsimiles of manuscripts and letters.

79 A map of days: life on the Left.
Denis Freney. Melbourne: Heinemann, 1991. 403p.

The autobiography of a schoolteacher and political activist, prominent in left-wing causes and campaigns in Sydney and overseas. He was born towards the end of the Depression years and raised in Sydney's southern suburbs near Botany Bay. He won a scholarship to Sydney University, where he graduated in history and began a teaching career. He joined the Communist Party, from which he was expelled for his anti-Stalinist views. He then joined the Trotskyites and became involved in revolutionary activities. Written in a light-hearted style, the book is an entertaining read and a valuable record of its times. A childhood spent in the Sydney suburbs, political activity at Sydney University, anti-Vietnam war demonstrations and anti-apartheid campaigns against the visiting South African Rugby team in 1971, are all vividly portrayed. Sadly, the book lacks an index.

80 Caddie: a Sydney barmaid: an autobiography written by herself.
Caddie, with an introduction by Dymphna Cusack. Melbourne: Sun Books, 1966. 199p.

First published in 1953, this is an autobiographical work published anonymously, but edited by well-known writer Dymphna Cusack. It is the story of a young woman who leaves her husband and has to fend for herself and her two young children during the 1930s Depression. The book is a tribute to the slum dwellers of inner Sydney who go out of their way to help Caddie. It also portrays humorously the social life and drinking rituals in the public houses, or pubs, where Caddie worked. A film of the book was produced in 1976. The film and the book effectively re-create inner-city Sydney life of the period.

81 Letters from Louisa: a woman's view of the 1890s, based on the letters of Louisa Macdonald, first principal of the Women's College, University of Sydney.
Jeanette Beaumont, W. Vere Hole. Sydney: Allen & Unwin, 1996. 202p. bibliog.

In 1892 a young Scotswoman arrived in Australia to become the first principal of the new Women's College at the University of Sydney. From 1891 to 1898 she wrote weekly letters to her friend and mentor in London, Eleama Grove. In this book extracts from the letters tell the story of the early days of the Women's College and offer an insider's view of life at the University and in Sydney during the 1890s. As principal of the Women's College, Louisa Macdonald was one of Sydney's leading women, and participated in almost every women's organization of the period. She was involved in campaigns for suffrage and against workplace exploitation and made a major contribution to the higher education of women. The book is an engaging account of the contribution of one of Australia's early feminists.

82   Maybanke Anderson: sex, suffrage & social reform.
Jan Roberts.   Sydney: Ruskin Rowe Press, 1997. 2nd ed. 240p.
bibliog.

Maybanke Susannah Anderson was born in England in 1845. She arrived in Sydney in 1855 with her parents and was educated as a teacher. She became involved in feminist issues, being an active suffragist, educator and social worker. She became a newspaper owner and editor and a published writer of history, contemporary social issues, newspaper articles and letters. In this book the author traces the life of her subject and her influential circle of friends, in the process giving an insight into the social conditions and concerns of Sydney society at the turn of the century.

83   Fanny to William: the letters of Frances Leonora Macleay 1812-1836.
Edited by Beverley Earnshaw and Joy Hughes with the assistance of Lindy Davidson.   Sydney: Historic Houses Trust of New South Wales and Macleay Museum, University of Sydney, 1993. 195p.
bibliog.

Frances Leonora (Fanny) Macleay's letters to her brother William Sharp Macleay span twenty-four years of the early 19th century. Fanny, born 1793, and William, born 1792, were the eldest daughter and son in a family of seventeen children born to Eliza and Alexander Macleay, a civil servant and entomologist. Fanny arrived in Sydney in January 1826 with her parents and five sisters when her father took up an appointment as Colonial Secretary of New South Wales. The family was soon involved in the social and philanthropic activities of Sydney's privileged society. Fanny's letters to her brother provide an entertaining account of her family, Sydney's social life and general living conditions in Sydney during the years 1826-37. The Macleays were a talented family involved in science and art. Elizabeth Windschuttle's *Taste and science: the Macleay women* (Glebe, New South Wales: Historic Houses Trust of New South Wales, 1988. 96p.) focuses on the women in the family as intellectuals involved in science, art, education, religion and philanthropy in Sydney during the first half of the 19th century.

84   Early Georgian: extracts from the journal of George Allen (1800-1877).
George Wigram Dundas Allen.   Sydney: Angus & Robertson, 1958. 136p.

George Allen arrived in Sydney at the age of fifteen in 1816 and later became the founder of Australia's earliest and longest-lived legal firm. Being a respected member of society, he was also active in religious circles, sat on company boards and was a prominent participant in municipal and political affairs. From the time of his arrival until shortly before his death in 1877 he kept a journal. His great-grandson has used the journal in a well-written biography, which also throws light on life and affairs of early 19th-century Sydney.

85   Mort's Cottage 1838-1988.
Jill Buckland.   Sydney: Kangaroo Press, 1988. 160p.

Mort's Cottage is a lovely, little Gothic stone cottage dating back to the beginnings of the Sydney harbourside suburb of Double Bay. When Jill Buckland moved into the cottage in

1979, she began to research the stories of all the people who had owned it, or the land on which it stood. This is a lively work and a detailed record of some of the most talented and notorious personalities in the history of Sydney. The book is splendidly illustrated with original artwork and photographs relating to the topics and people discussed in the text.

History

General

86   Sydney: a biography of a city.
Lucy Hughes Turnbull.   Sydney: Random House, 1999. 534p.
bibliog.

A big book which focuses on significant social and political events that have shaped the city from a penal settlement to one of the world's most desirable and glamorous cities, the home of the Olympic Games in the year 2000. The second part of the book concentrates on the physical components of the city and suburbs by placing them in a historical and cultural context. Throughout the book there are interesting contemporary illustrations. There is also an extensive, up-to-date bibliography.

87   Sydney: a story of a city.
Shirley Fitzgerald.   Sydney: City of Sydney, 1999. 169p. maps.
bibliog.

This large-format book is published to coincide with the production of a film of the same name, commissioned by the City of Sydney, and directed by Geoff Burton and Bruce Beresford, for the giant Imax screen in Sydney. It measures thirty-eight metres wide and twenty-eight metres high and is the biggest cinema screen in the world. The book combines images from the film with historical photographs of Sydney and commentary to offer the reader a visual and verbal insight in how the city developed.

88   The Sydney scene 1788-1960.
Arranged and introduced by Alan Birch, David S. Macmillan.
Sydney: Hale & Iremonger, 1982. 387p. bibliog.

This is a well-chosen collection of more than 200 extracts from contemporary documents and other writings, such as newspapers and books, evoking the atmosphere of Sydney between 1788 and 1960. It is a reprint of a book first published in 1962. The book is divided into five chronological periods, each preceded by the compiler's commentary on social, economic and political developments and on the art and literature of the time. It is

24

illustrated with contemporary prints and photographs. It is excellently suited for browsing, to gain an insight into what made the city what it is today.

89   10,000 years of Sydney life: a guide to archaeological discovery.
Edited by Peter Stanbury with the assistance of Judy Birmingham.
Sydney: The Macleay Museum, The University of Sydney, 1979.
123p. bibliog.

A collection of essays divided into two sections: pre-1788, or before white settlement; and after 1788. This book, published to coincide with a Sydney Unearthed exhibition at the Macleay Museum, is a good introduction to Sydney history and archaeology.

90   Secrets in stone: discover the history of Sydney.
Geoff Stuart.   Sydney: Brandname Properties, 1993. 268p. bibliog.

Sydney lies on a sandstone plateau, which was heavily quarried during the early years of settlement. Although other local material has been used in buildings throughout the city as well, sandstone is certainly the most prolific. Author and photographer Geoff Stuart recreates Sydney's history by looking at Sydney buildings and stone constructions from 1788 to the present by means of 300 colour photographs and linking text.

91   This was Sydney: a pictorial history from 1788 to the present time.
Suzanne Mourot.   Sydney: Ure Smith, 1969. 155p. maps. bibliog.

At the time of writing, the author was the Deputy Mitchell Librarian at the Public Library of New South Wales. For this book she has chosen 217 illustrations from the Library's collection – paintings, sketches, lithographs, prints and photographs – to depict Sydney's beginnings, the way it looked, the way it grew and how it developed into the modern metropolis it is today. The illustrations are supported by contemporary extracts, written by people who knew the city intimately at its various stages of development. Overall, it is a pictorial history of Sydney that is most delightful for browsing.

92   First views of Australia 1788-1825: a history of early Sydney.
Tim McCormick and others.   Sydney: David Ell Press in association with Longueville Publications, 1987. 340p.

The first book to comprehensively document and catalogue all known views of the first settlement in Australia – Sydney – from 1788 to 1825. Many of the works are held in private collections or museums, not easily accessible, and are illustrated here for the first time. The book not only provides a record of the early art of Australia, it is a chronological pictorial record of the built environment of Sydney during its first thirty-seven years.

93   Sydney takes shape: a collection of contemporary maps from foundation to federation.
Max Kelly, Ruth Crocker.   Sydney: Doak Press in association with The Macleay Museum, The University of Sydney, 1978. 2nd ed. 49p.

A collection of twenty-four maps which cover the years between the first settlement at Sydney Cove and the solidly suburban Sydney of the 1890s. They illustrate the rapid physical spread of the city and the text attempts to isolate some of the topographical and economic characteristics of this spread. Thus in 1861 Sydney contained twenty-seven per cent of the population of New South Wales; by 1891 this percentage had risen to thirty-five and by 1911, to forty-seven.

94   Seaport Sydney: the makings of the city landscape.
Peter Proudfoot.   Sydney: UNSW Press, 1996. 311p. maps. bibliog. tables.

This book presents a detailed analysis of the historical evolution of Sydney Harbour. The author maintains that significant city growth has always been preceded by major port and maritime construction about a decade earlier. As the argument is based on a study of maps, there is a comprehensive bibliography appended of ninety maps held in the Mitchell Library in Sydney, relating to the development of the city of Sydney and its harbour and port.

95   The Rocks: life in early Sydney.
Grace Karskens.   Melbourne: Melbourne University Press, 1997. 304p. maps. bibliog.

The Rocks, on the western side of Sydney Cove or Circular Quay, as it is known today, has the longest history of any post-1788 settlement. In this, the first scholarly history of the Rocks, the author covers in great detail every aspect of the rich community life of the area from 1788, when it was a convict settlement, up to 1840. For a wealth of excellent illustrations the reader is referred to Max Kelly's *Anchored in a small cove: a history and archaeology of The Rocks, Sydney* (Sydney: Sydney Cove Authority, c1997. 119p.). This book had its origins in the exhibition in the Sydney Visitors Centre in the Rocks. It is a thematic social history, richly illustrated with historic pictures and artefacts.

96   Inside the Rocks: the archaeology of a neighbourhood.
Grace Karskens.   Sydney: Hale & Iremonger, 1999. 240p. maps. bibliog. plans.

For twenty weeks in 1994 a team of archaeologists, together with some 400 volunteers, excavated a site between Cumberland and Gloucester Streets in Sydney's Rocks area. This site represents an extraordinary material record of past urban life in Sydney. The book takes the reader inside the everyday life of the area over the late 18th and 19th centuries. Maps and photographs complement this fascinating narrative about Rocks people, their houses and possessions and the neighbourhood they created.

97   Sydney's highways of history.
Geoffrey Scott.   Melbourne: Georgian House, 1958. 263p. bibliog.

A popular history of life in Sydney through an examination of the buildings, many now demolished, and personalities of Sydney's main thoroughfares. Written by a journalist, the book is very readable.

98 Sydney's streets: a guide to Sydney City street names.
Shirley Fitzgerald. Sydney: Sydney City Council, 1995. 122p.
maps. bibliog.

A dictionary of street names for Sydney and the inner suburbs from 1842 onwards. It identifies street names and gives their derivations. It covers the Central Business District (from Circular Quay to Central Railway Station) and the surrounding areas of Pyrmont, Ultimo, Darlinghurst, Woolloomooloo, Chippendale, Surry Hills, Paddington and the Rocks. Useful maps and photographs accompany the text.

99 Historical records of New South Wales.
Edited by F. M. Bladen. Sydney: Government Printer, 1893-1901. 7 vols.

This series of historical documents contains mainly despatches and enclosures from the early Governors to the Colonial Office authorities in England. They cover the years 1780-1811 and provide primary source material for the early history of Sydney and New South Wales. They were republished by Lansdown Slattery in 1978-79. Also relevant are the *Historical Records of Australia,* published in thirty-three volumes by the Library Committee of the Commonwealth Parliament from 1914 to 1925. They overlap some of the material in the New South Wales series, but continue the documents up to 1848.

Foundation to 1800

100 Australia: the first twelve years.
Peter Taylor. Sydney: Allen & Unwin, 1982. 220p. bibliog.

A popular account of the first twelve years of settlement, 1788-1800, based on the recorded experiences of the early colonists. It is a fascinating story of how an isolated community, six months' sailing away from the mother country and consisting of soldiers, civil officers and British criminals, survived to lay the foundations of today's Australia. At the end of the twelve-year period Sydney had grown into a town with a harbour, the surrounding interior had been explored and farming was established. On a sadder note, the seeds of conflict with the Aborigines had been sown as well.

101 Phillip of Australia: an account of the settlement at Sydney Cove 1788-92.
M. Barnard Eldershaw. Sydney: Angus & Robertson, 1977. 366p. bibliog.

A reissue of the book, first published in 1938 as a collaborative effort by Marjorie Barnard and Flora Eldershaw, under a common form of their names. This is probably still one of the best written accounts of the first years of life in Sydney, not least because it is written by authors who bring to history their combined talents as novelists. As well as considering the achievements of Phillip, the first Governor of New South Wales, the book examines the untouched environment surrounding Sydney and aspects of life in the colony such as law, religion, exploration and the contact between whites and Aborigines.

The book combines thorough documentation with the best kind of historical imagination and is recommended to anyone with an interest in Sydney's beginnings. The authors also collaborated on novels set in Sydney: *A house is built* and *Green memory*.

102 Buried alive, Sydney 1788-1792: eyewitness accounts of the making of a nation.
Jack Egan.   Sydney: Allen & Unwin, 1999. 351p. bibliog.

Sydney's first white settlers were convicts, soldiers and clerks, many of whom have left behind diaries, letters, journals and paintings. With a minimum of editorial linking the compiler has gathered these eye-witness accounts and placed them in chronological order to give the reader a vivid picture of the first five years of a new colony. Short biographies of the contemporary contributors accompany the source material.

103 Sydney Cove 1795-1800: the second Governor.
John Cobley.   Sydney: Angus & Robertson, 1986. 622p.

This is the fifth and final volume under the *Sydney Cove* title. The first covers the events of 1788 (published in 1962), the second 1789-90 (published in 1963), the third 1791-92 (published in 1965), the fourth 1793-95 (published in 1983), and now the fifth 1795-1800. At the time of publication in 1986, the previous four volumes were republished in a uniform set. This story of the first twelve years of Sydney's settlement is told entirely through the diaries and letters of the officers and settlers. The excerpts set down the minutiae of life on a new continent: births, deaths, baptisms and settlers' accounts of their encounters with Aboriginals, snakes, lightning, meteors, storms, accidents and disasters. The result is extremely vivid and fresh. It is remarkable that Cobley is not a professional historian, but a retired physician.

104 1788: comprising A narrative of the expedition to Botany Bay and A complete account of the settlement at Port Jackson.
Watkin Tench, edited and introduced by Tim Flannery.   Melbourne: Text Publishing, 1996. 276p.

Tench was a captain of the marines when he arrived in Australia with the First Fleet in 1788. He had had a literary education and possessed a natural curiosity which caused him to write two compelling accounts of the infant colony: *A narrative of the expedition to Botany Bay* (1789) and *A complete account of the settlement at Port Jackson* (1793). Generally recognized as the best of the First Fleet narratives, this latest is a popular edition. A scholarly edition of Tench's books was published by L. F. Fitzhardinge in 1979. The book is a powerful evocation of the early struggles to establish the settlement at Port Jackson, later renamed Sydney.

105 An account of the English colony in New South Wales.
David Collins, edited by Brian H. Fletcher.   Sydney: Reed in association with The Royal Australian Historical Society, 1975. 2 vols. bibliog.

The original edition, which appeared in two successive volumes in 1798 and 1802, has long enjoyed a reputation as one of the major sources of early Australian (Sydney) history. Its author, secretary to the first Governor Arthur Phillip and responsible for the colony's legal establishment, is sometimes described as the first historian of New South

Wales. To counter a negative English view of the new colony, Collins gave an optimistic account. He was sympathetic to the plight of the Aborigines, whose customs he described, and fully acknowledged the harm done them by the Europeans. The conditions and happenings at Sydney are described in great detail in good prose.

106 The origins of Australian capital cities.

Edited by Pamela Statham. Cambridge, England: Cambridge University Press, 1989. 364p. maps. bibliog.

This collection of papers by specialists presents a comparative view of the origins of Australia's eight capital cities. Two chapters are devoted to Sydney, 1: *The founding of New South Wales*, by Ged Martin and 2: *Sydney: a southern emporium*, by Brian Fletcher. The first deals with site selection and the second with the process of post-settlement growth.

107 The foundation of Australia (1786-1800); a study in English criminal practice and penal colonization in the eighteenth century.

Eris O'Brien. Sydney: Angus & Robertson, 1950. 2nd ed. 327p. bibliog.

A classic work which was first published in 1937. It is in two parts: the first covers the discussions in England about establishing a penal colony in Australia; and the second deals systematically and in great detail with the main subject, the actual foundation of the colony at Sydney Cove.

108 1788: the people of the First Fleet.

Don Chapman. Sydney: Doubleday, 1986. 191p. bibliog.

This book contains brief biographies of the over 1,300 people – military, naval, civic and convicts – who sailed to Australia in the First Fleet. In effect, these are the founding fathers and mothers of Australia and the first inhabitants of the new settlement of Sydney. There are a number of black-and-white contemporary illustrations.

109 The founders of Australia: a biographical dictionary of the First Fleet.

Mollie Gillen with appendices by Yvonne Browning, Michael Flynn, Mollie Gillen. Sydney: Library of Australian History, 1989. 608p. bibliog.

This is a monumental reference work comprising biographies of all the persons who reached Sydney Cove in January 1788. It is based on twenty years' research in the archives and records relating to the First Fleet and shows that the founders were not homogeneous but presented a rich multicultural mix: as well as English, Irish, Scottish and Welsh there were at least fourteen North Americans, at least twelve black Africans or West Indians, at least nine Jews and people from Holland, France, Germany, Norway, Sweden, India and other places.

110 A bibliography of the First Fleet.

Victor Crittenden. Canberra: Australian National University Press, 1981. 359p.

This bibliography embraces the history of the First Fleet's voyage to Australia and the period of the first settlement at Sydney Cove until the arrival of the second fleet in June 1790. It covers the period starting with the proposals to form a settlement in the South Pacific, but more specifically, with the proposal by James M. Matra in 1785 up to June 1790.

111 The second fleet: Britain's grim convict armada of 1790.

Michael Flynn. Sydney: Library of Australian History, 1993. 787p. bibliog.

During the voyage to Australia of the First Fleet (1787-88) only 22 convicts died out of a total of 755. In stark contrast twenty-six per cent of the 1,006 convicts on board died before the Second Fleet reached Sydney and forty per cent had perished eight months later. Michael Flynn tells the story of the Second Fleet in great detail. By far the greater portion of the book consists of biographies of the 1,500 convicts, seamen and soldiers who sailed with the Fleet and settled in Sydney or nearby. During the 1790s, however, many of them were sent to Norfolk Island.

112 A difficult infant: Sydney before Macquarie.

Edited by Graeme Aplin. Sydney: NSWU Press, 1988. 169p.

Produced by the Sydney History Group which was formed in 1975 to encourage interest in Sydney's history. The book contains a collection of essays by historians who focus on Sydney before 1810. The year 1810 was a milestone in the history of the township. When Governor Lachlan Macquarie took office on 1 January 1810, stability returned to the government of the young colony for the first time since Governor Arthur Phillip left for England in December 1792. The intervening period treated in this volume represented a period of infancy: a difficult, boisterous and often undernourished and undisciplined time.

113 Collins, the courts & the colony: law & society in colonial New South Wales 1788-1796.

J. F. Nagle. Sydney: UNSW Press with funding assistance from the Law Foundation of New South Wales and Charles Sturt University, 1996. 337p. bibliog. (The Modern History Series).

The book draws on original court records to examine the judicial career of Australia's first legal officer – Deputy Judge Advocate, Captain David Collins, a man without any formal legal qualifications. The author does not merely describe the everyday tasks of dispensing justice, but vividly reconstructs the life and times, conflicts, alliances, developments and values at work in a new society centred on Sydney. The author served for twenty-three years as a member of the New South Wales Supreme Court bench.

114 The first Fleet Marines, 1786-1792.

John Moore. Brisbane: University of Queensland Press, 1987. 345p. bibliog. tables.

The author has written this work mainly to provide an account of life in the first four years of Sydney from the viewpoint of the First Fleet marines. These naval soldiers were sent to protect the British colony at Botany Bay and maintain its law and order. It is as much a contribution to social as to military history. The text is based on contemporary diaries and other unpublished sources. There are appendices which list the members of the Corps, biographies of the officers and a list of children born on board the First Fleet and in Sydney. There is a centre set of illustrations, notes, a bibliography and an index.

19th century

115 Nineteenth century Sydney: essays in urban history.
Edited by Max Kelly.   Sydney: Sydney University Press in association with the Sydney History Group, 1978. 135p. maps. bibliog.

This is the first publication by the Sydney History Group, which was formed by specialists in diverse fields in order to research and discuss the history of Sydney. Contributions for this book are drawn from a range of disciplines among which figure geography, demography, architecture, politics and history, and which reflect the variety of perspectives from which Sydney's past may be viewed. There are two valuable chapters on historical source material: one concerned with the State Archives of New South Wales; and the other a select bibliography of Sydney during the period 1800-1900. In 1980 the Group issued a second volume, *Twentieth century Sydney: studies in urban and social history* (see item no. 122).

116 The age of Macquarie.
Edited by James Broadbent, Joy Hughes.   Melbourne: Melbourne University Press in association with Historic Houses Trust of New South Wales, 1992. 194p. bibliog.

Lachlan Macquarie was Governor of New South Wales from 1810 to 1821. During those years Sydney flourished. When his governorship ended, the convict settlement became a civil colony with most legal and economic restrictions removed. The book contains eleven essays by historians who explore various aspects of the development of the colony during those years. Colonial society, imperial policy, the economy, religion and education are discussed in detail. There are several essays dealing with material culture: literature and music, art, furniture and its makers, silver and silversmithing and the architecture of public buildings, many of which are still standing today. This is an excellent introduction to a most significant period in early colonial history.

117 Rum rebellion: a study of the overthrow of Governor Bligh by John Macarthur and the New South Wales Corps.
H. V. Evatt.   Sydney: Angus & Robertson, 1978. 365p. (Australian Classics).

In January 1808 Major Johnston and the officers of the New South Wales Corps, urged on by wealthy merchant, pastoralist and ex-member of the Corps, John Macarthur, made an armed attack on Government House in Sydney, arrested Governor William Bligh and took control of the Colony. Evatt, a distinguished statesman, High Court Judge and Cabinet Minister, using original documents, including court records, characterizes the only coup in Australia's history as a clash between a colonial élite of wealthy settlers and the military on one side, and the more numerous small settlers who were favoured by Bligh on the other. The author comes to the conclusion that Bligh was the champion of the small settlers and puts the blame on the élitists. M. H. Ellis's 1955 biography of Macarthur robustly supports the rebels, while Ross Fitzgerald and Mark Hearn re-examine the rebellion in their book *Bligh, Macarthur and the rum rebellion* (Kenthurst, New South Wales: Kangaroo Press, 1988. 144p.).

118 The battle of Vinegar Hill: Australia's Irish rebellion, 1804.
Lynette Ramsay Silver. Sydney: Doubleday, 1989. 168p.

The book examines in great detail a revolt of Irish convicts, which led to a clash between them and troops, assisted by free settler volunteers, on 5 March 1804 near Parramatta on the outskirts of Sydney. Australia's first rebellion was of brief duration and resulted in the death by shooting of about fifteen rebels, the subsequent hanging of nine, with various others undergoing flogging. The author also examines the old feud between the Irish and the English and Catholic versus Protestant, in this case transferred to the Antipodes.

119 Life in the cities: Australia in the Victorian age, Vol.3.
Michael Cannon. Melbourne: Viking O'Neil, 1988. 320p. bibliog.

This is the third volume covering Australia during the Victorian Age (1837-1901). *Who's master? Who's man,* and *Life in the country,* are the first two volumes. Volume 3 is up to the same high standard as the first two and deals with the astounding growth of Australian cities during the latter part of the 19th century. Although each capital city is included, the emphasis is on the two larger ones, Melbourne and Sydney. This book is recommended to the general reader for its readability and informative content. It is social history at its best.

120 Gaslight Sydney.
Louise Johnson. Sydney: Allen & Unwin, 1984. 112p. bibliog.

This book presents the history of Sydney in the late 19th century – the gaslight era, between 1875 and 1900. The volume consists of a well-balanced mixture of the author's own text and contemporary photographic and written documents: excerpts from materials by travellers, investigative reporters, novelists and businessmen. It is a vivid snapshot of Sydney at a particular stage in its development.

20th century

121 Sydney since the twenties.
Peter Spearritt.   Sydney: Hale & Iremonger, 1978. 294p. maps.
bibliog.

The story of Australia's largest and most cosmopolitan city during the period of its
greatest growth, from 1920, when Sydney was a 'walking-distance' city, to the 1970s,
when it had been transformed into a sprawling metropolis. The author is a lecturer in
urban studies. In this book he has not only produced a study of the development of the
city, but also tells the story of fashion and mode of life enjoyed by the population of the
day. The painstakingly collected photographs, cartoons, sketches and maps bring the text
to life and reproduce the flavour of Sydney for the resident and the visitor alike. An
extensive bibliography accompanies the text.

122 Twentieth century Sydney: studies in urban and social history.
Edited by Jill Roe.   Sydney: Hale & Iremonger, 1980. 272p. maps.
bibliog. plans.

The second collection of studies by specialist authors about the history of Sydney by the
Sydney History Group. It follows *Nineteenth century Sydney: essays in urban history,*
edited by Max Kelly (see item no. 115). Collectively, the studies attempt to locate the
diverse forces shaping the modern city of Sydney and the life of its people. This work will
be of interest to architects, geographers, planners, political scientists, as well as historians
and all people concerned with the urban environment.

**123 Battle surface: Japan's submarine war against Australia 1942-
44.**
David Jenkins, with maps and graphics by Peter Sullivan.   Sydney:
Random House, 1992. 304p. bibliog.

During the Second World War Japan mounted forty submarine missions around Australia
and New Zealand, sinking seventeen merchant ships. They caused many deaths and
shocked Australians into the realization that the war had come home, especially when
midget submarines penetrated Sydney Harbour in 1942 and sank the converted ferry
Kattabul, killing twenty-one naval ratings. This book is well researched – using Japanese
official archives, interviews with Japanese survivors and Allied records – and gives a
detailed account of the submarine campaign against Australia. Other works on this
subject are: *Midget submarine attack on Sydney* by Lew Lind (Garden Island, New South
Wales: Bellrope Press, 1990. 72p.); and *Australia under siege: Japanese submarine
raiders 1942* by Steven L. Carruthers (Sydney: Solus Books, 1982. 192p.).

Suburban

124 Sydney's suburbs: how and why they were named.
Ken Anderson. Sydney: Kangaroo Press, 1989. 80p. maps.
600 Sydney suburbs are listed in alphabetical order with maps for locating them. The origin of the name is given in a short paragraph for each locality. The book is based on a series which first appeared in the *Daily Telegraph* newspaper. There is no indication of the sources used.

125 The book of Sydney suburbs.
Compiled by Frances Pollon, original manuscript by Gerald Healy.
Sydney: Angus & Robertson, 1988. 288p. bibliog.
Arranged in alphabetical order, this book is a compilation of short histories of more than 400 Sydney suburbs. It includes over 200 black-and-white pictures, a useful bibliography and an index of people mentioned in the text. It is intended as a quick reference for the layman. A very similar book, but concentrating on only forty municipalities extant at the time and with more extensive text, is Brian and Barbara Kennedy's *Sydney and suburbs: a history & description* (Frenchs Forest, New South Wales: Reed, 1982. 158p.).

126 Sydney: city of suburbs.
Edited by Max Kelly. Sydney: New South Wales University Press in association with the Sydney History Group, 1987. 213p. maps.
bibliog. plans.
A collection of papers based on the theme that the heartland of Sydney exists in its suburbs and the characteristic Sydney experience has been in and of the suburb. The book explores some of these experiences. To this end, types of Sydney suburbs – the garden suburb, the railway suburb, the owner-builder suburb, the élite suburb and the red brick suburb of the 1920s – have been chosen for discussion.

127 Bondi.
Robert Drewe and others. Sydney: Allen & Unwin, 1993. new ed.
96p.
Bondi symbolizes Sydney. The long sweep of Bondi Beach with its summer crowds of thousands of sun and surf worshippers is often cited as proof of the hedonistic lifestyle of Sydneysiders. However, Bondi is more than simply a beach. It is an area full of life and energy. It is a cosmopolitan suburb and is the home of working-class Australians, trendy young executives, Jewish people, Italians, New Zealanders, Greeks, Hungarians, Lebanese and Vietnamese. In this book some of Australia's most talented writers and photographers pay tribute to Bondi. It is a loving survey of an area that has become a legend.

128 Pyrmont & Ultimo under siege.
Shirley Fitzgerald, Hilary Golder. Sydney: Hale & Iremonger,
1994. 134p. maps.
This is the last book of six on inner city localities, which form part of the Sydney City Council's History Project, created to mark the sesquicentenary of local government in

Sydney in 1992. All these books, written by specialists, represent a large advance on the local histories of old with their monotonous recitation of facts. These studies place the local area in the larger society. There is also a successful marrying of text, illustration and documentation which adds to the reader's understanding of the subject.

129 Miller's Point: the urban village.
Shirley Fitzgerald, Christopher Keating.   Sydney: Hale & Iremonger, 1991. 128p. maps.

This is volume three of the Sydney History Project and follows the high standards set by the other volumes, both in research and in the presentation of information, with illustrations ably supplementing the text. Miller's Point is perhaps best known today as the location of the district known as the Rocks, one of the earliest settlement at Sydney Cove. What was once a close-knit working-class suburb has today become a tourist area of shops, galleries and restaurants adjacent to the city's Central Business District.

130 Marrickville: people and places.
Chris Meader, Richard Cashman, Anne Carolan.   Sydney: Hale & Iremonger, 1994. 200p. maps. bibliog. tables.

This volume is a continuation of the authors' publication *Marrickville: rural outpost to inner city* (Petersham, New South Wales: Hale & Iremonger, 1990. 224p.), and has been arranged to complement the first volume. It covers themes such as transport, communications, religion, education, culture and recreation in this sprawling 'inner west' municipality of Sydney. It is the epitome of modern multicultural Australia, being the home of Greek, Vietnamese, Lebanese, Portuguese, Yugoslav, Korean, Irish, Scottish, English, Islander and Aboriginal ethnic minorities. These social histories are distinguished by quality research and lively writing and are of a much higher standard than the run-of-the-mill 'cut and paste' local histories. The large number of contemporary illustrations add to the pleasure of the book.

131 Surry Hills: the city's backyard.
Christopher Keating.   Sydney: Hale & Iremonger, 1991. 120p.

A richly illustrated social history of the inner suburb of Surry Hills, commissioned as part of the Sydney City Council's sesquicentenary series of books on Sydney and its immediate neighbourhoods. Like most of Sydney's inner suburbs, what was once a working-class area has in recent years become gentrified as the middle classes have moved in to enjoy the benefits of inner-city living. It is a very multicultural area with a large Lebanese population.

132 Chippendale: beneath the factory wall.
Shirley Fitzgerald.   Sydney: Hale & Iremonger, 1990. 120p. maps.

A social history of Chippendale – old Sydney's working-class heart – in the excellent City of Sydney's Sesquicentenary History Project.

133 Larrikin days: 100 years of growing up in an Australian suburb.
Tony Stephens with Annette O'Neill. Sydney: Nicholson Street
Public School Parents and Citizens Association in association with
John Ferguson, 1983. 112p. bibliog.

The book started life as a project to celebrate the centenary of a school in Balmain, a
famous inner-city working-class suburb, which in recent years has seen a rebirth as a
haven for artists and young professionals. The book finished up as a rich collection of
reminiscences and recollections by a diverse group of people. Boxers, fishermen,
shopkeepers, soldiers, dressmakers, local politicians, state politicians, teachers, thieves,
actresses and sailors all recall and recount their experiences. The result makes fascinating
reading, as it presents a slice of suburban social history 'from below'. Interesting
photographs of people and places accompany the text. For more photographs of Balmain
and its inhabitants the reader should consult *The Balmain book* by David Liddle, a local
photographer (Leura, New South Wales: Second Back Row Press, 1985. 112p.).

134 Paddock full of houses: Paddington 1840-1890.
Max Kelly. Sydney: Doak Press, 1978. 208p. maps. plans. tables.
diagrams.

The book tells of the development of 400 acres of steep, difficult land, five kilometres
from the city centre, from a village to a densely populated commuter suburb. The author
deals with the basic realities involved in making a suburb – land sales, building practices,
water and sewerage, street lighting, rates, mortgages, kerbing and guttering and public
transport – but does not neglect the human element and describes the birth places and
religions, the jobs, the marriage patterns and family size, the homes and the hobbies of
the local residents. He shows how by 1890 Paddington was a self-conscious and proud
community, although twenty years later it was well on the way to becoming a first-class
slum. Today it is again gentrified, populated by the upwardly mobile professional classes
who prefer inner-city living.

**135 Leichhardt: on the margins of the city: a social history of
Leichhardt and the former municipalities of Annandale,
Balmain and Glebe.**
Max Solling, Peter Reynolds. Sydney: Allen & Unwin, 1997.
314p. maps. bibliog. tables.

This large-format, well illustrated, thematic history of Leichhardt, a municipality
covering twelve square kilometres just to the west of Sydney's Central Business District,
is an authoritative and well-written account. It traces the development of the area from
Aboriginal beginnings, through war, depression and immigration, to the turbulent times
of resident action and community participation in the 1970s and 1980s to the present. Like
most inner-suburban areas of Sydney since the late 1960s, the residential character of
Leichhardt has been transformed as more and more professional and other white-collar
workers have displaced the former blue-collar inhabitants. A process of 'gentrification'
has taken place.

136   Kings Cross album: pictorial memories of Kings Cross, Darlinghurst, Woolloomooloo & Rushcutters Bay.
Elizabeth Butel, Tom Thompson.   Sydney: Atrand, 1984. 123p. bibliog.

The book is a pictorial record with commentary of the changes, over time, in the built environment of the near-city suburbs of Kings Cross, Darlinghurst, Woolloomooloo and Rushcutters Bay. Once the area was a calm retreat, dotted with the gracious houses and splendid gardens of some of the most wealthy and influential people in the colony of New South Wales. The 20th century saw many of these houses subdivided and new terrace housing built. The cheap rents attracted a large number of artists, writers and actors to the area, which became attached to a bohemian lifestyle earlier than any other area in Sydney.

137   North Sydney 1788-1988.
Michael Jones.   Sydney: Allen & Unwin, 1988. 304p. maps. bibliog. tables.

The present history is not a straight chronological narrative of the development of North Sydney, but rather a thematic account, looking at North Sydney from the broader perspective of urban development. Although North Sydney is only a short distance from the Sydney downtown area, the 500-metre barrier of the Harbour caused it to develop differently from the rest of the metropolis. Until the completion of the Harbour Bridge in 1932, there was little local industry and most residents commuted by ferry to work across the Harbour waters. The opening of the Harbour Bridge did not bring the desired improvements expected by most residents. There were major problems and a twin downtown Central Business District slowly developed with high-rise buildings and traffic congestion. This is a scholarly, well-illustrated and interesting history of a unique part of the Sydney metropolitan area.

138   Mosman: a history.
Gavin Souter.   Melbourne: Melbourne University Press, 1994. 378p. maps. bibliog.

A detailed, narrative history of the middle-class suburb of Mosman, a peninsula on the northeastern shore of Sydney Harbour. Written by an award-winning historian, the book is a cut above the run-of-the-mill local history.

139   Mosman impressions.
Text by Nancy Phelan, photographs by Mark Lang, Phillip Ramsden, Philip Quirk.   Sydney: Mosman Municipal Council, 1993. 163p.

Creative, imaginative people have always been drawn to Mosman, a jagged peninsula in Sydney Harbour, where the beaches and wilderness still abound, although it is only a short distance from prosperous suburbia and within half an hour of the city of Sydney. Nancy Phelan, a successful writer herself, has compiled a book of excerpts from writers and art works from painters as well as artistic photography from the writers and artists who have lived or visited Mosman since its beginnings as a whaling station in the 1830s. It is a fascinating, finely produced, large-format volume, made for browsing to gain an impression about Sydney's harbourside.

140 **Holroyd: a social history of Western Sydney.**
Grace Karskens. Sydney: New South Wales University Press, 1991. 280p. bibliog.

A history of the Municipality of Holroyd which lies about twenty kilometres west of Sydney, halfway between the city and the Blue Mountains. Today, Holroyd lies close to the demographic epicentre of the Sydney metropolitan area, but in the rapid growth period after the war, the unfashionable western suburbs were regarded as almost the edge of the world. Many illustrations accompany the text.

141 **Parramatta: a past revealed.**
Terry Kass, Carol Liston, John McClymont. Sydney: Parramatta City Council, 1996. 454p. maps. bibliog.

Parramatta was the second settlement in Australia after Sydney, of which it is now a suburb in the western region of the metropolitan area. It is twenty-four kilometres by road west of Sydney at the head of the Parramatta River, a large tidal estuary of Sydney harbour. This exhaustive history of the area from European settlement to the present updates and supersedes the previous standard history, James Jervis's *The cradle city of Australia* (Sydney: Parramatta City Council, 1961. 234p.).

142 **Bankstown: a sense of identity.**
Sue Rosen. Sydney: Hale & Iremonger, 1996. 185p. maps. bibliog.

This well-illustrated and researched book traces the physical, social and economic development of the Bankstown area from prehistory to the 1990s. It was published to celebrate the centenary since Bankstown was proclaimed a Municipal district in 1895, and fifteen years since Bankstown was accorded city status in 1980. Bankstown is twelve kilometres from Sydney.

143 **On the frontier: a social history of Liverpool.**
Christopher Keating. Sydney: Hale & Iremonger, 1996. 226p.

A richly-illustrated social history of Liverpool, located thirty-five kilometres southwest of Sydney and founded by Governor Macquarie in 1810. It started as a small country town and became an outer suburb of Sydney on the frontier between the metropolitan area and the country and also served as a frontier for social experiment.

Flora, Fauna and Geology

144 **Taken for granted: the bushland of Sydney and its suburbs.**
Doug Benson, Jocelyn Howell.   Sydney: Kangaroo Press in
association with the Royal Botanic Gardens Sydney, 1995. 160p.
maps. bibliog.

This book describes the impact of Sydney's growth on its original natural vegetation,
from European settlement in 1788 to the present day. Today, only small patches of the
original bushland remain. Many of these areas are in parks and reserves, but careful
management is needed if they are to survive. The major part of the book consists of an
examination of the vegetation of each of Sydney's forty local council areas. The authors
are plant ecologists with Sydney's Royal Botanic Gardens. The book is profusely
illustrated with colour and black-and-white photographs.

145 **Field guide to the native plants of Sydney.**
Les Robinson.   Sydney: Kangaroo Press, 1994. 2nd ed. 448p.
bibliog.

This is a user-friendly guide for the identification of Sydney's native plants. Over 1,370
species are illustrated with line drawings and the text includes information on the history,
ecology, Aboriginal and European uses of each plant, together with references to
literature and the journals of explorers. A much more convenient book, of a handy size to
fit in a hiker's knapsack, is *Sydney flora: a beginner's guide to native plants,* by Tony
Edmonds and Joan Webb (Sydney: Surrey Beatty, 1998. 2nd ed. 156p.).

146 **Native plants of the Sydney district: an identification guide.**
Alan Fairley, Philip Moore.   Sydney: Kangaroo Press in association
with The Society for Growing Australian Plants, 1989. 432p. maps.
bibliog.

This is an identification guide to the native plants of the Sydney region, an area which
extends from Newcastle to Nowra on the eastern seaboard, and west to the Great Dividing
Range. It contains colour photographs and descriptions of about 1,500 species and is the
result of over twelve years of research and photographic forays in search of both common

and rare species of plants. Written in a simplified, readable style with a necessary minimum of botanical terms, it contains a full range of plants from ferns, herbs, sedges and grasses to shrubs and trees, many of which are illustrated for the first time. Alan Fairley has scientific qualifications and is an enthusiastic hiker with books on bushwalking to his credit.

147 Flora of the Sydney region.
N. C. W. Beadle and others.   Sydney: Reed Books, 1986. 722p. bibliog.

This is a reprint with alterations of the completely revised 1982 edition, which has become the standard work on the flora of the Sydney region, taking in the central coastal regions between Nowra and Newcastle, to the adjacent Great Dividing Range to the west. Brief descriptions of all the plant species are provided. Line drawings and photographs offer additional aid to identification and there is a glossary, list of references and an extensive index. The author is one of Australia's foremost botanists.

148 The Royal Botanic Gardens, Sydney: a history 1816-1985.
Lionel Gilbert.   Melbourne: Oxford University Press, 1986. 210p. bibliog.

The Royal Botanic Gardens of Sydney are located on a site of thirty hectares adjoining the magnificent Sydney Harbour and the Central Business District of the city. Its beginnings lay in the Government Farm begun only seven months after the First Fleet arrived at Sydney Cove in 1788. Thus the site marks the first stirrings of agriculture and botany in Australia and has remained the main centre of enquiry and information relating to the plant species of New South Wales. It is also a haven for visitors, both local and from overseas. Dr Gilbert has written an entertaining history of the Gardens, which will be enjoyed by any botanist or plant lover.

149 The best of wildlife in the suburbs.
Densey Clyne, illustrated by Martyn Robinson.   Melbourne: Oxford University Press, 1993. 243p.

These essays, accompanied by charming drawings by Martyn Robinson, are based on the author's popular column in *The Sydney Morning Herald,* which depicts the wildlife found in the average suburban garden and backyard: birds, insects, spiders and other animals. Clyne is the author of twenty-two books on natural history subjects and a contributor of articles and photographs to Australian and overseas magazines.

150 The birds of Sydney, County of Cumberland, New South Wales 1770-1989.
E. S. Hoskin.   Sydney: Surrey Beatty, 1991. 2nd ed. 289p. bibliog.

This book was intended to be a total revision of the 1958 edition of *The birds of Sydney,* written by K. A. Hindwood and A. R. McGill, published by the Royal Zoological Society of New South Wales, but for various reasons has been extended far beyond the scope of that book. The book includes 447 species of birds sighted in the Sydney region out of an Australian total of 799 recorded species. The guide also suggests where to see birds in Sydney, lists the species which are becoming rare and discusses the feeding habits of birds. There is a helpful chapter on how to distinguish birds of similar appearance.

151   Frogs and reptiles of the Sydney region.
Ken Griffiths.   Sydney: UNSWP, 1997. 125p. bibliog.

Of the 750 species of reptiles found in Australia, a little over 100 species occur in the Sydney region. This book is a comprehensive photographic field guide to the frogs, snakes, lizards and tortoises living in the greater Sydney area. There are detailed descriptions of size, colour, habits, preferred habitats and, for the snakes, potential danger. Information is also provided on the treatment and prevention of snake bites. The purpose is to allow for ready identification of all species. Handily pocket-sized, the guide is an ideal companion for the keen hiker or bush walker.

152   Beauty and the beasts: a history of Taronga Zoo, Western Plains Zoo and their antecedents.
Ronald Strahan.   Sydney: Zoological Parks Board of New South Wales in association with Surrey Beatty, 1991. 160p.

Taronga Zoo is spectacularly situated on thirty-two hectares of ground on the north shore of Sydney Harbour, a short ferry ride from downtown Sydney. An Aerial Cabin Ride takes visitors from the ferry to the top of the Zoo, giving panoramic views of the Zoo, the harbour and the city beyond. It is the home for almost 4,000 animals of 700 species and highlights unique Australian flora and fauna. It receives over one million visitors a year. This book presents the history of the zoo from its antecedents in the 19th century run by the Zoological Society and the Acclimatization Society, its opening in 1916 and to the early 1990s. Strahan is an academic zoologist who was the Director of Taronga Zoo from 1967 to 1974.

153   Sydneyside scenery and how it came about (Also Canberra and Kosciusco).
Griffith Taylor.   Sydney: Angus & Robertson, 1958. 239p. maps.

Professor Griffith Taylor, an eminent geologist and geographer, provides a description of Sydney to explain the geological background to the topography of today, and at the same time outlines the history of Sydney and shows how geography and topography have combined to determine the pattern of that history. The style of writing is clear and concise and the numerous maps, diagrams and illustrations aid understanding.

Population

Aborigines

154 The Aborigines of the Sydney district before 1788.
Peter Turbet.   Sydney: Kangaroo Press, 1989. 160p. bibliog.

A readable, introductory text on the traditional life and culture of the Aborigines who inhabited the Sydney area before the arrival of the white settlers in 1788.

155 When the sky fell down: the destruction of the tribes of the Sydney region 1788-1850s.
Keith Willey.   Sydney: Collins, 1979. 231p. bibliog.

When Captain James Cook landed on the east coast of Australia in 1770, Sydney and its environs was the permanent home of seven tribes of Aborigines, numbering about 3,000 individuals. Eighty years later they were all dead. In that period they had been exterminated either directly by the white settlers, from disease or through the destruction of their environment and forms of communal life. This book provides a comprehensive account of the fate of the Aboriginal tribes of the Sydney region.

156 Bennelong: first notable Aboriginal: a report from original sources.
John Kenny, design and layout by Ian C. Cox.   Sydney: Royal Australian Historical Society in association with the Bank of New South Wales, 1973. 73p.

Documents the life of Bennelong, an Aboriginal captured in 1789, who became a friend of Governor Phillip and travelled with him to London, where he met King George III at St. James. The publication of this monograph was timed to coincide with the opening of the Sydney Opera House on Bennelong Point, which is named after this 'notable Aboriginal'. For the same reason Isadore Brodsky published *Bennelong profile* (Sydney: University Co-operative Bookshop, 1973. 95p.) at the same time.

157 King Bungaree: a Sydney Aborigine meets the great South Pacific explorers 1799-1830.
Keith Vincent Smith.   Sydney: Kangaroo Press, 1992. 192p. maps. bibliog.

Bungaree (?-1830), an Aboriginal from the Broken Bay, New South Wales region, was well known in early 19th-century Sydney, after his arrival there in the 1790s. He accompanied Matthew Flinders on the *Investigator* which circumnavigated Australia in 1801-02. Bungaree was witty and intelligent and was for many years a Sydney 'character', dressed in cast-off European military clothes, often mentioned in contemporary accounts of the colony and often painted or sketched. This book traces the life of Bungaree and throws much light on the early life of Sydney. The book is richly illustrated, especially interesting being the many sketches and paintings of Bungaree.

158 Guests of the Governor – Aboriginal residents of the first Government House.
Isabel McBryde.   Sydney: The Friends of the First Government House Site, 1989. 62p. bibliog.

This paper was originally delivered as the Third Foundation Day Lecture held by the Friends of the First Government House Site at the University of Sydney in 1986. Based on original research by the distinguished author, an eminent academic and Foundation Member of the Australian Institute of Aboriginal Studies, the lecture illuminates the lives of individual Aboriginal people in contact with the early occupants of First Government House and their social circle. On a wider plane, it is an insightful essay in race relations. The text is enhanced by forty-one plates of contemporary pictorial material.

159 The Darug and their neighbours: the traditional Aboriginal owners of the Sydney region.
James Kohen.   Sydney: Darug Link in association with Blacktown and District Historical Society, 1993. 300p. bibliog.

Essentially, this is a family history tracing the genealogies of several western Sydney Aboriginal families. However, there are also valuable descriptions of traditional life – clan structure, economy and ceremonial life – together with an extensive vocabulary of the local Aboriginal languages.

160 The Parramatta Native Institution and the Black Town: a history.
J. Brook, J. L. Kohen.   Sydney: New South Wales University Press, 1991. 295p. bibliog.

The arrival of the white settlers in 1788 at Sydney Cove immediately produced a cultural clash with the original inhabitants – the Aborigines. One of the methods of resolving the conflict was the process of 'civilising the Aborigines', which is dealt with in this book. The School for Aborigines was established in 1814 to educate children in the 'three Rs'; it was subsequently relocated to an area that became known as the Black Town and still exists today as Blacktown. Descendants of those original Aborigines still inhabit the area today. The original Native Institution ended in failure and had ceased to exist by 1832.

161   The Russians at Port Jackson 1814-1822.
Glynn Barratt.   Canberra: Australian Institute of Aboriginal Studies,
1981. 114p. bibliog.

The book very methodically examines the extent of Russian interest in New Holland, as Australia was known in the early 19th century. The author, Professor of Russian at Carleton University in Ottawa, Canada, has studied archives and original documents in several Russian depositories, where he was specifically concerned with ethnographic observations of the Aboriginals. He includes the observations of nine naval officers who visited Sydney and were particularly interested in Aborigines' material culture and physical appearance. The volume is well-organized with finely reproduced illustrations of Aborigines from the Sydney region.

**162   A field guide to Aboriginal rock engravings with special
reference to those around Sydney.**
Peter Stanbury, John Clegg with poems by David Campbell.
Melbourne: Oxford University Press, 1996. 163p. maps. bibliog.
tables.

This book provides practical information, maps, sketches and photographs to easily accessible sites of Aboriginal rock engravings in the Sydney area, which has more prehistoric rock art than any other city in the world. David Campbell's poems about the carvings evoke the spirituality of Aboriginal Australia.

163   The Sydney language.
Jakelin Troy.   Canberra: Australian Dictionaries Project and the
Australian Institute of Aboriginal and Torres Strait Islanders Studies,
1993. 116p. maps. bibliog.

The author wrote the book to revive interest in a long extinct Aboriginal language of the Sydney district and to make available the small amount of surviving information about the language. The language has also been known as Dharug and Iyora. The book includes many illustrations to help the reader visualize the Sydney Aborigines, their technology, cultural life and physical environment. Another scholarly work on the Sydney language is Paul Carter's *The calling to come* (Sydney: Historic Houses Trust of New South Wales, 1996. 82p.).

Other ethnic groups

164   Cosmopolitan Sydney: explore the world in one city.
Jock Collins, Antonio Castillo.   Sydney: Pluto Press with
Comerford and Miller, 1998. 491p.

One out of three Sydneysiders, or over one million people, were born overseas or are first-generation migrants. They represent more than 150 nationalities. This detailed guide covers food, nightlife, cafés, sport, shopping, media and the cultural events of all of the major ethnic groups in Sydney. It also gives background information on the various groups. This is an excellent city guide for overseas visitors to the 2000 Sydney Olympic Games.

165 Minorities: cultural diversity in Sydney.
Edited by Shirley Fitzgerald, Garry Wotherspoon.   Sydney: State Library of New South Wales Press in association with the Sydney History Group, 1995. 216p. bibliog.

Sydney is a culturally diverse city which has been profoundly enriched by the contributions of its many ethnic communities. This collection of essays by members of the Sydney History Group explores some of the different minorities in Sydney which have influenced its culture, society and politics. The emphasis is on the Greek, Italian, Jewish, Aboriginal and gay communities.

166 Red tape, gold scissors: the story of Sydney's Chinese.
Shirley Fitzgerald.   Sydney: State Library of New South Wales Press in association with the City of Sydney, 1997. 206p. bibliog.

This book by the well-known historian of Sydney, based on extensive research and scores of interviews with Chinese families, traces the long and rich history of the Chinese in Sydney.

167 Pages of history: a century of the Australian Jewish Press.
Suzanne Rutland.   Sydney: Australian Jewish Press, 1995. 303p.

A detailed historical study of the Jewish press and the Jewish community that supported it. *The Australian Jewish News,* the oldest Jewish newspaper in Australia, has been published in Sydney for over 100 years and has been an institution for the Sydney Jewish community, which today numbers over 100,000 members. Many black-and-white photographs illustrate the text. The same author published *Seventy-five years: the history of a Jewish newspaper* (Sydney: Australian Jewish Press, 1970. 107p.). This is exclusively devoted to the *Australian Jewish Times,* incorporating the *Hebrew Standard,* and devotes a lot of space to a discussion of the Jewish community in Sydney.

168 The house of Israel.
Israel Porush.   Melbourne: The Hawthorn Press, 1977. 347p.

A study of Sydney Jewry from its foundation in 1788 and a history of the Great Synagogue of Sydney, the mother congregation of Australian Jewry, compiled on the occasion of its centenary (1878-1978). The author was Rabbi of the Great Synagogue from 1940 to 1972, as well as an author and contributor of historical articles to the *Journal of the Australian Jewish Historical Society.*

169 From pasta to pavlova: a comparative study of Italian settlers in Sydney and Griffith.
Rina Huber.   Brisbane: University of Queensland Press, 1977. 270p. bibliog.

A sympathetic and informative study, from an anthropological perspective, of the differing circumstances confronting immigrants from one area of Italy. The author, a sociologist, has studied eight Trevisani families in Sydney and compared them with the settlement of Trevisani in Griffith, a rural irrigation area in New South Wales. The book shows how the adjustment to their different environments has led to two different life-styles.

170 Greek children in Sydney.
Eva Isaacs.   Canberra: Australian National University Press, 1976. 128p. (Immigrants in Australia, no. 6).

A research study on the experience of Greek children of school age in Sydney and their difficulties of adjusting and fitting into the Australian school environment. This study is part of a series on immigrants sponsored by the Academy of the Social Sciences in Australia.

Religion

171 A place in the city.
Edmund Campion.   Melbourne: Penguin Books, 1994. 188p.
The author, a Catholic intellectual, recalls living in and around St. Mary's Cathedral in Sydney. He reflects on the varied people associated with the Cathedral, their connections with the wider church and their sense of Australian identity. Finally, the book unfolds as a celebration of Sydney, both in its contemporary reality and in its historical development. In a sense, this book is a sequel to Campion's *Rockchoppers: growing up Catholic in Australia* (Melbourne: Penguin Books, 1982. 241p.), which reflects on the author's and the wider Catholic experience of education from school to Sydney University in the early 1950s.

172 Sydney Anglicans: a history of the Diocese.
Stephen Judd, Kenneth Cable.   Sydney: Anglican Information Office, 1987. 393p. bibliog.
The Church of England in Australia became the Anglican Church of Australia on 24 August 1981. Traditionally it had been the largest religious denomination in Australia. Due to immigration and other factors, it has recently fallen behind the Roman Catholic Church in total membership. This is a history of the Sydney Anglicans from the start of the penal colony in 1788 to the present day.

173 Truly feminine, truly Catholic: a history of the Catholic Women's League in the Archdiocese of Sydney 1913-87.
Hilary M. Carey.   Sydney: NSWU Press, 1987. 218p. bibliog.
A critical study of that characteristic women's organization, the church auxiliary. While other women's organizations have embraced changed attitudes to the role and status of women, the Catholic Women's League has remained steadfastly and proudly conservative, supporting the clergy, raising money and upholding a cherished and increasingly threatened view of the home, family and society. This book gives an insight into a Sydney which is very different from its popular image as a hedonistic society.

174   These women?: women religious in the history of Australia, the Sisters of Mercy, Parramatta 1888-1988.
Madeleine Sophie McGrath.   Sydney: New South Wales University Press, 1989. 301p. bibliog.

A scholarly book by a nun in the Order about which she writes; however, as she says, her history is not a 'triumphal presentation of the glories' of this religious order, but an attempt to 'situate them within the history of the Church and women's history in the wider community'. The author traces the transformations in the work and living practices of the nuns caused by the changes in Vatican and Australian government policies. The links she draws between Church and State, religion and politics, particularly in the area of the nuns' involvement in education and welfare, makes the book rather more than a mere record of the lives of nuns.

175   Yesterday's seminary: a history of St. Patrick's, Manly.
K. J. Walsh.   Sydney: Allen & Unwin, 1998. 380p.

Commissioned to mark the closure of St. Patrick's College in the seaside suburb of Manly, the book provides a detailed, critical account of the history of Catholic clerical education over 170 years. The focus is on the leaders rather than the students, recognizing the aspirations towards intellectual rigour that saw the seminary, at times, proclaimed as the precursor of a Catholic university. During its existence the seminary took exactly 100 ordination classes to priesthood.

Society and Social Conditions

176   Sydney: a social atlas.
Gregory W. Bray: Regional Director.   Canberra: Australian
Government Publishing Service, 1998. 85p. maps.

This *Social atlas* is one of a series of atlases of Australian capital cities produced by the
Australian Bureau of Statistics. It contains maps illustrating a range of social,
demographic and economic characteristics of the population of Sydney, using data
collected in the 1996 Census of Population and Housing. A commentary accompanying
each map briefly analyses these characteristics and highlights the main features. Censi are
taken every five years, for example 1991, 1986, 1976 and 1971, and social atlases have
been published on the data collected in these earlier surveys.

177   Out west: perceptions of Sydney's western suburbs.
Diane Powell.   Sydney: Allen & Unwin, 1993. 187p. bibliog.

The western suburbs of Sydney comprise about half of Sydney's geographic area and are
home to more than forty per cent of the city's population. Over many years a belief has
arisen, propagated by the media and residents of more affluent areas of Sydney and New
South Wales generally, that the inhabitants of this mostly working-class area – the
'westies' – are unsophisticated and indeed rather stupid. This book investigates the myth
and finds that 'westies' are resourceful and innovative, and have developed their own
intricate social and cultural networks. *Home/World: space, community and marginality in
Sydney's West*, by Helen Grace and others (Annandale, New South Wales: Pluto Press,
1997. 204p.), is an exploration of the same topic from a theoretical viewpoint.

178   Sex and anarchy: the life and death of the Sydney Push.
Anne Coombs.   Melbourne: Viking, 1996. 340p. bibliog.

Throughout the 1950s and 1960s the Sydney Push was a Bohemian and anarchic network
of Sydneysiders who frequented pubs, liked the races and enjoyed a good argument. The
men and women of the Push were against the State, the Church, teetotalling puritans and
censorship. They experienced the sexual revolution fifteen years before the rest of
Australian society. At its centre were the Sydney Libertarians, followers of the tough-

minded, empirical philosophy of Sydney University's Professor John Anderson and his Freethought Society. Another work on the Sydney Push is by Judy Ogilvie, who spent her early twenties among its members. She has set down her 'impressionist memoirs' in *The Push: an impressionist memoir* (Sydney: Primavera Press, 1995. 182p.).

179 A Sydney gaze: the making of gay liberation.
Craig Johnston. Sydney: Schiltron Press, 1999. 275p.

The author is a Sydney gay activist and social commentator. This book is a collection of some of his newspaper and journal articles, speeches and conference papers and 'calls to arms' that he wrote from 1973 to 1998. The writings indicate some key issues facing the gay movement and gay community in Sydney at particular times in their histories. Sadly there is no index.

180 'City of the plain': history of a gay subculture.
Garry Wotherspoon. Sydney: Hale & Iremonger, 1991. 256p.

Using conventional historical sources and oral history, the author traces the major changes in Sydney's homosexual sub-cultures since the 1920s. An earlier book on the subject is Denise Thompson's *Flaws in the social fabric: homosexuals and society in Sydney* (Sydney: Allen & Unwin, 1985. 192p.).

181 Being a prostitute: prostitute women and prostitute men.
Roberta Perkins, Garry Bennett. Sydney: Allen & Unwin, 1985. 318p. bibliog.

Like other large cities of the world, Sydney has a long history of prostitution. However, this is the first study giving detailed accounts of the perceptions and experiences of a variety of prostitutes, male and female, homosexual and heterosexual, of different ages and backgrounds. The authors have personal knowledge of the current nature of prostitution in Sydney through their work with gay youths and transsexuals. The data they collected includes both survey material and in-depth interviews and the book focuses on twenty-one individual cases. For a brief historical survey of prostitutes in Sydney, the reader is referred to Roberta Perkins' 'Working girls in "wowserville": prostitute women in Sydney since 1945', in *Australian welfare: historical sociology*, edited by Richard Kennedy (Melbourne: Macmillan Australia, 1989, p. 362-89).

182 A history of the Sydney Gay and Lesbian Mardi Gras.
Graham Carbery. Melbourne: Australian Lesbian and Gay Archives, 1995. 281p. tables.

Sydney's Gay and Lesbian Mardi Gras annual festival has become known as a visual spectacle without equal, with over half a million people watching the parade. However, behind the colour and glamour lies a long history of struggle and confrontation with the authorities and the 'moral majority'. This book provides a detailed account of the development of the most popular gay and lesbian event in the world.

183 Mardi Gras!: true stories.
Edited by Richard Wherrett. Melbourne: Viking, 1999. 252p.

The Sydney Gay and Lesbian Mardi Gras is currently Australia's largest gay and lesbian organization, supported by 7,400 voting members, thirteen full-time staff, five part-time workers and approximately 1,500 volunteers. The month-long Mardi Gras festival, held in Sydney during February, is made up of over 100 events and is the largest gay and lesbian festival in the world. More than half a million people watch the Parade, which has over 200 entries. A further one million people watch the delayed telecast. Just under 40,000 people attend the Mardi Gras Party and Sleaze Ball. The present book presents a grassroots history of the event. Editor Richard Wherrett, one of Australia's foremost theatre directors, has put together 102 stories, mostly by participants, which vary as much in style and subject as in ideology, in order to evoke the history and atmosphere of the festival.

184   Faces of the street: William Street, Sydney, 1916.
Max Kelly.   Sydney: Doak Press, 1982. 174p. bibliog.

In 1916 the Sydney City Council decided to widen the south side of William Street, which connects the city with Darlinghurst, to turn the street into a grand boulevard – the Champs Elysées of Sydney. This book is a social study of William Street at the time. An anonymous photographer had photographed all ninety-four condemned properties and Kelly, using rate books and other documents, creates a social history of the times by delving into the street life of 1916 – a world of pubs and poverty, grocers and pawnbrokers, prostitutes and boarding-house keepers. The buildings shown in the photographs also represent a virtual catalogue of colonial building styles from 1830 to 1900. Today, the street remains a nondescript commuter road lined with car show-rooms, scarcely worth the human and architectural cost of the original intention of the city fathers.

185   Representing the slum: popular journalism in a late nineteenth century city.
Alan Mayne.   Melbourne: History Department, The University of Melbourne, 1991. 187p. bibliog. (Melbourne University History Monograph Series, no. 13).

The book consists of newspaper extracts from the 1880s relating to Sydney's slums and the social conditions prevailing there, according to the newspaper reports. The author, a lecturer in comparative urban history, has written a long introductory essay to indicate how these 'primary sources' should be interpreted by historians 100 years later. The book provides an insight not only for the sociologist, but also for the general reader into the social conditions of the working classes in late 19th-century Sydney.

186   The hatch and the brood of time: a study of the first generation of native born white Australians 1788-1828. Volume I.
Portia Robinson.   Melbourne: Oxford University Press, 1985. 369p. bibliog.

This controversial book based on rarely-used sources re-creates the first generation of white settlers in New South Wales and focuses on Sydney during the forty years following settlement. The native-born Australians are individually identified and set in the wider context of colonial development. The portrait of life that emerges is entirely different from that depicted in accounts which emphasize the depraved convict background.

187 The women of Botany Bay: a reinterpretation of the role of women in the origins of Australian society.
Portia Robinson.   Melbourne: Penguin Books, 1993. 494p. bibliog.

First published in 1988, this pioneering study has now been reissued in paperback. The book tells the story, backed by detailed research, of the convict women and wives of convicts transported to New South Wales and centred on Sydney during the first forty years of white settlement. Robinson demolishes the official view that these women were 'filthy whores' beyond restoration to society. She shows that most became respectable family members and working women who were never again convicted of even minor offences or misdemeanours.

188 Living in cities: urbanism and society in metropolitan Australia.
Edited by Ian Burnley, James Forrest.   Sydney: Allen & Unwin and the Geographical Society of New South Wales, 1985. 273p. maps. bibliog. tables.

Australia is a highly urbanized society in which seventy per cent of the population lives in cities of 100,000 or more inhabitants. Their urban lifestyle is the subject of this collection of multi-disciplinary essays, with most of the examples and data drawn from the Sydney metropolitan area. This volume of essays, written for the Geographic Society of New South Wales, deals with the social dimension of urbanism, just as a companion volume *Why cities change*, edited by Richard V. Cardew, John V. Langdale, David C. Rich (Sydney: Allen & Unwin and the Geographical Society of New South Wales, 1982. 307p.), looked at processes of economic change, with particular reference to Sydney.

189 The Journalists' Club, Sydney: a fond history.
Don Angel.   Sydney: The Journalists' Club, 1985. 200p.

An informal story of the first forty-six years of the Journalists' Club. Having many writers and artists among its members, the Club was known for its literary and artistic activities, such as frequent addresses by local and overseas visiting celebrities. The author knows the Club intimately: he was its President for thirteen years, 1953-57 and 1967-76, and a Club director for twenty-three years.

190 The Union Club.
Roy H. Goddard, decorations by L.C. Hudson.   Sydney: Halstead Press, 1957. 140p.

Founded in the British tradition as a Gentlemen's club, the Union Club has been a venue for the Sydney and country establishment to the present day. The Union Club is housed in a substantial building in Bent Street and is conducted along the conservative lines of its English models.

Health and Welfare

191   Times of crisis: epidemics in Sydney 1788-1900.
P. H. Curson.   Sydney: Sydney University Press, 1985. 195p. maps.
bibliog. graphs. tables.

A scholarly study about the effects of a number of traumatic epidemics of infectious
diseases which affected Sydney during the period 1788-1900. Although the six epidemics
discussed in this book killed relatively few people, they incapacitated many thousands
and created a climate of bewilderment, panic and resentment. Dr Curson also shows how
these epidemics highlighted the unsanitary living conditions of Sydney's poor and were a
prime cause of public health reform.

**192   Fever, squalor and vice: sanitation and social policy in Victorian
Sydney.**
A. J. C. Mayne.   Brisbane: University of Queensland Press, 1982.
263p. maps. bibliog. tables.

This is a penetrating analysis of Sydney's 19th-century slum problem. The inner city
working-class areas were overcrowded and crime-ridden, with public hygiene practically
non-existent. Mayne traces the history of the fitful campaigns of 19th-century doctors and
politicians to cleanse the slums and elevate their people. It is, as the author describes it, a
story of muddled thinking, bureaucratic inertia and political indifference. The only large-
scale slum clearances followed a series of smallpox outbreaks in the late 1870s and early
1880s, carried out due to the fear that fevers generated by the 'filth and squalor of the
poor' would 'extend to the rich'.

193   Plague in Sydney: the anatomy of an epidemic.
Peter Curson, Kevin McCracken.   Sydney: New South Wales
University Press, 1989. 213p. maps. bibliog. tables. graphs.

The 1900 epidemic of bubonic plague in Sydney was one of Australia's greatest social
disasters. Although only 303 cases and 103 deaths were officially reported, the epidemic
caused widespread social and economic disruption and profoundly affected the lives of
thousands of Sydneysiders. This scholarly study of the epidemic is the definitive work on

the subject. For dramatic photographs of the period of the epidemic the reader should consult *Plague Sydney 1900*, edited by Max Kelly (Sydney: Doak Press, 1981. 100p.).

194 Medicine and madness: a social history of insanity in New South Wales 1880-1940.
Stephen Garton.   Sydney: New South Wales University Press, 1988. 212p. bibliog.

A scholarly study based on rich archival sources in the New South Wales Lunacy Department. The sources include hospital cases, records and correspondence by doctors, superintendents and patients. The emphasis throughout the book is on mental care in Sydney, since the only available hospital records are for three institutions in Sydney.

195 In quarantine: a history of Sydney's Quarantine Station 1828-1984.
Jean Duncan Foley.   Sydney: Kangaroo Press, 1995. 160p. bibliog.

The Quarantine Station was established at North Heads entrance to Sydney Harbour in 1828. The author tells of the privations endured by the 572 people who died and the 13,000 who languished in quarantine during the following 156 years. In 1984 the establishment was declared redundant and the area it occupied became a national park. The book brings to life the history of immigration and the development of public health administration in Australia. A list of the names, where known, of people who died and/or were buried at the Quarantine Station during the period 1837-1962 appears at the end of the book.

196 The heart of the city: the first 125 years of the Sydney City Mission.
June Owen.   Sydney: Kangaroo Press, 1987. 219p. bibliog.

Voluntary social agencies have played a major role in Australian society. In this book the author traces the history of one of these agencies, the Sydney City Mission, and shows its aims, achievements and failures, and how it has interacted with the people of Sydney since its founding in 1862. Based primarily on the Mission's own records, the book traces its 19th-century British origins as part of a movement both to evangelize the poor and to relieve their suffering. This joint evangelical and welfare mission is increasingly hard to maintain in a society which today is becoming more secular and critical and the author argues for a changed role for the Mission in the future.

197 A very present help: caring for Australians since 1813: the history of the Benevolent Society of New South Wales.
Ron Rathbone.   Sydney: State Library of New South Wales Press, 1994. 237p.

The Benevolent Society of New South Wales was formed in 1818 with the aim to provide 'relief of the poor, aged and infirm and for other benevolent purposes'. From the formative years of the colony until the early part of this century, when the government became involved in the provision of social services, the Benevolent Society was the major private, religiously inspired, provider of assistance and support for the disadvantaged in society. It was responsible for establishing many institutions in Sydney to carry out its aims, including the Benevolent Asylum, Renwick Hospital for Infants, the Scarba Welfare

House for Women and Children and, most notable of all, The Royal Hospital for Women which was founded in 1862. When administration of the hospital was handed over to the government in 1992, this had been the longest and most remarkable example of service to women and children by a private organization that Australia had ever seen. This large-format book with many illustrations is a comprehensive account of the organization's 175 years of existence, written by a director of the Society since 1972, and President since 1993.

198 A century of caring: the Royal North Shore Hospital 1888-1988.
Geoffrey Sherington, with assistance from Dr Roger Vanderfield. Sydney: Horwitz Grahame in association with Royal North Shore Hospital, 1988. 189p.

A centenary history of one of Sydney's major hospitals. Although this is essentially a history of the changing administration of the hospital, set against the emerging system of health care in New South Wales, the author, a staff member of the Faculty of Education at the University of Sydney, has interwoven some of the social and political history of the North Shore community. The book is copiously illustrated with photographs.

199 'The Royal': a history of the Royal Hospital for Women 1820-1997.
Ian Cope, William Garrett. Sydney: The Royal Hospital for Women, 1997. 209p. bibliog.

The story of the Royal Hospital for Women is intimately linked with that of the Benevolent Society of New South Wales. It reflects the development of maternity services in the colony and the State of New South Wales and the changes in the social conditions of Sydney over the last 175 years. When the government took over the administration of the hospital in 1992, this brought to an end the longest association of a private charitable organization – The Benevolent Society – with the running of a major hospital. The author served as Honorary Obstetrician and Gynaecologist at the hospital for many years. The book is illustrated with black-and-white photographs.

200 Hand in hand: the story of the Royal Alexandra Hospital for Children, Sydney.
D. G. Hamilton. Sydney: John Ferguson, 1979. 338p. bibliog.

This is the centenary history of Sydney's Royal Alexandra Hospital For Children, written from the Hospital's records by a long-time senior employee of the hospital. As well as being an institutional history, the book also details the changes in children's diseases over 100 years, the great advances made in paediatric medicine and surgery, and the progressive establishment within the hospital of the modern treatment and research units to cope with children's diseases. Many black-and-white illustrations accompany the text.

201 Children of the back lanes: destitute and neglected children in colonial New South Wales.
John Ramsland. Sydney: NSWU Press, 1986. 249p. bibliog.

There were hordes of neglected children roaming the streets of Sydney in the early colonial period. In accordance with the views of the authorities, these children were rounded up and institutionalized and taught the values of the colonial élite: morality, industry, moderation, cleanliness, sobriety, frugality, service and the Christian way. The book is a scholarly study of the various institutions or orphanages set up during the 19th century to reform destitute and neglected children and the controversies which surrounded the ideological goals and the methods of the various schemes.

202   The quick and the dead: a biomedical atlas of Sydney.
John B. Gibson, Arne Johansen.   Sydney: Reed, 1979. 152p. bibliog.

The authors have produced computer-generated maps of Sydney suburbs showing high and low risk areas for the diseases which kill eighty-six per cent of Sydney's women and eighty-nine per cent of men. Sydney's three major killers, which caused more than half the annual deaths in the late 1970s, were heart disease, cancer and strokes and the situation has not changed much in the late 1990s.

203   A history of dentistry in New South Wales 1945-1995.
George Franki.   Sydney: Dental Board of New South Wales and Australian Dental Association (New South Wales Branch), 1997. 304p.

This history of the dental profession in Sydney and New South Wales brings up to date an earlier work, *A history of dentistry in New South Wales 1788 to 1945*, compiled and edited by R. W. Halliday and A. O. Watson (Sydney: Dental Board of New South Wales and Australian Dental Association [New South Wales Branch], 1977. 261p.). Dental organizations and societies, the faculty of Dentistry at the University of Sydney and dental hospitals in Sydney are treated in great detail. There is an interesting account of the struggle to introduce fluoridation of the public water supplies, and biographies of many of the men and women who played important roles in the events are featured throughout the text.

Education

204 **Sydney and the bush: a pictorial history of education in New South Wales.**
Jan Burnswoods, Jim Fletcher.   Sydney: New South Wales Department of Education, 1980. 259p.

This pictorial record of education in New South Wales commemorates the centenary of the State's Department of Education. Most of the illustrations have come from the Department's own collection, but other institutions have also contributed.

205 **The first generation: school and society in early Australia.**
John F. Cleverley.   Sydney: Sydney University Press, 1971. 168p. bibliog.

A detailed account of the beginnings and early development of education in the penal colony of New South Wales, particularly during the period 1788-1809. The author presents a clear account of predominant educational ideas in England at the time of white settlement and of early colonial conditions in and around Sydney. Although the emphasis of the book is upon educational efforts, throughout there is an informative description of various aspects of early Sydney society.

206 **Two centuries of education in New South Wales.**
Alan Barcan.   Sydney: New South Wales University Press, 1988. 352p. bibliog.

A chronological, academic history of 200 years of education in New South Wales, including Sydney. The book was first published in 1965 as *Short history of education in New South Wales*. It is disappointing that there are only some sixty pages to give an account of the complicated period of educational change after 1965 in the present book. Moreover, the bibliography has not been updated.

207   Australia's colonial culture: ideas, men and institutions in mid-nineteenth century eastern Australia.
George Nadel.   Melbourne: Cheshire, 1957. 304p. bibliog.

This book is not concerned with the artistic or aesthetic aspects of culture, but rather with what people in the 19th century called 'the machinery of intellectual and moral improvement'. The author tells of efforts to plant knowledge more widely and reap social unity and national sentiment in Eastern Australia around the middle of the 19th century. The centre of attention of the book, however, is the colony of New South Wales and Sydney.

208   Her natural destiny: the education of women in New South Wales.
Noeline Kyle.   Sydney: NSWU Press, 1986. 251p. bibliog.

Based on the author's doctoral thesis, the book reviews the period 1788-1920 to establish what educational provisions were made for girls and how and why they differed from those provided for boys. Based on research in a wide variety of primary and secondary sources, the work surveys government, denominational and private schools and home education at primary and secondary levels. There are also chapters on industrial and technical training and on the training of women teachers.

209   Education in New South Wales: a guide to state and Commonwealth sources 1788-1992.
Christabel Wescombe, Geoffrey Sherington.   Sydney: Hale & Iremonger, 1993. 192p.

A comprehensive bibliography of education in New South Wales, which confines itself to official publications.

210   Australia's first: a history of the University of Sydney.
Sydney: The University of Sydney in association with Hale & Iremonger, 1991-95. 2 vols. bibliog.

A comprehensive, scholarly history of Australia's first university from the time of its formation in the mid-19th century to 1990. Volume 1 by Clifford Turney, Ursula Bygott and Peter Chippendale covers the years 1850 to 1939, and volume 2 by W. F. Connell and others deals with the period 1940-90. There are many historic photographs and the text is documented in great detail. A companion volume has been published, entitled *Australia's first: a pictorial history of the University of Sydney 1850-1990* by Kenneth Cable, Clifford Turney and Ursula Bygott (Sydney: University of Sydney, 1994. 128p.).

211   Sydney University Monographs.
Series editor: C. Turney.   Sydney: University of Sydney, 1985- .

The University History Research Project was established in 1975, its main task being the publishing of a comprehensive history of the University: *Australia's first,* completed in two volumes in 1995 (see previous item). The Project Committee has also undertaken to publish this series of monographs on individual university personalities, institutions, buildings and events. Eight monographs on these topics had been published by 1993.

212 History at Sydney 1891-1991: centenary reflections.

Edited by Barbara Caine and others. Sydney: History Department, University of Sydney, 1992. 239p.

A set of individual essays written by current members of the History Department to commemorate the work of the Department at its centenary. The emphasis is on what students had studied, rather than on the administrative aspects of the Department's history. Further information on the study of history in New South Wales and Sydney, not only in academia but within the school curriculum, is provided in Brian H. Fletcher's *Australian history in New South Wales 1888-1938* (Kensington, New South Wales: NSW University Press, 1993. 228p.).

213 A century down town: Sydney University Law School's first hundred years.

Edited by John Mackinolty, Judy Mackinolty. Sydney: Sydney University Law School, 1991. 272p. bibliog.

A comprehensive history, the chapters being contributed by various Faculty members. An earlier publication is *The jubilee book of the Law School,* edited by Sir Thomas Bavin (Sydney: [Law School, University of Sydney?], 1940. 246p.).

214 Ever reaping something new: a science centenary.

Edited by David Branagan, Graham Holland. Sydney: University of Sydney Science Centenary Committee, 1985. 256p. bibliog.

A centenary history of science at the University of Sydney and the development of the Faculty of Science written by members of the Faculty. Another book on a more specific subject is *The Messel era: the story of the School of Physics and its Science Foundation within The University of Sydney, Australia 1952-1987,* edited by D. D. Millar (Sydney: Pergamon Press, 1987. 157p.). It marks the retirement of the flamboyant Professor Harry Messel as Head of the School and as Director of the Science Foundation.

215 Centenary book of the University of Sydney Faculty of Medicine.

Edited by John Atherton Young, Ann Jervie Sefton, Nina Webb. Sydney: Sydney University Press for the University of Sydney Faculty of Medicine, 1984. 548p. bibliog.

A well-illustrated book which traces the development of the Faculty of Medicine from its initial, non-teaching role in the 1850s to its present distinguished position. A companion volume, *Centenary book of the Medical Society of the University of Sydney* (Sydney: Hale & Iremonger, 1992. 224p.), presents the students' perspectives on events, people and places.

216 The history of the Women's College within the University of Sydney.

W. Vere Hole, Anne H. Treweeke. Sydney: Halstead Press, 1953. 211p.

Women were first admitted to the University of Sydney in 1881. In 1892 the Women's College opened in temporary premises in Glebe, moving to its own building within the University grounds in 1894. This book presents a detailed history of the College's first sixty years. In 1995 the Council of the Women's College published a *Biographical register: the Women's College within the University of Sydney. Volume 1: 1892-1939*, compiled and edited by the College Archivist, Rosemary Annable. This book contains detailed biographies of the College Council, staff and students. It is intended to continue the register to the present.

217 Finishing school for blokes: college life exposed.
Peter Cameron. Sydney: Allen & Unwin, 1997. 201p.

The author was Principal of St. Andrew's College, one of the oldest male residential colleges of the oldest university in Australia, the University of Sydney. He was appointed in 1991, but resigned in 1995, after increasing disillusionment with a system he found himself unable to alter. He reveals a conservative institution dominated by rituals of a culture based on sport, alcohol, and 'fresher' initiations, manoeuvrings of the Council of prominent businessmen, and the archaic and narrow attitude to women as equal partners in the education process. The book is a fascinating insider's view of a part of Australia's traditional culture, which has produced many pillars of the establishment.

218 The Andrews book: St. Andrew's College within the University of Sydney.
R. Ian Jack. Sydney: Principal and Councillors of St. Andrew's College, 1989. 3rd ed. 159p.

A history of St. Andrew's, a Presbyterian residential college, the third of the collegiate foundations within the University of Sydney, established in 1870. The author is Senior Fellow, Archivist and Librarian at the College. He has also published *St. Andrews College 1870-1995: the first 125 years in photographs* (Sydney: St. Andrew's College, University of Sydney, 1995. 128p.).

219 A passion to oppose: John Anderson, philosopher.
Brian Kennedy. Melbourne: Melbourne University Press, 1995. 234p. bibliog.

John Anderson (1893-1962) was Australia's most important philosopher in the first half of the 20th century. He was born in Scotland and educated at the University of Glasgow. After appointments in Cardiff, Glasgow and Edinburgh, he came to the Challis Chair of Philosophy at the University of Sydney in 1927 and held it until his retirement in 1958. He became a key intellectual influence in Sydney's wider society. During the late 1940s he inspired Sydney's Libertarian Push, a loose association of intellectuals who met in cafés and pubs for drinking and discussion and took part in social issues campaigns of the day. The book is a sympathetic treatment of the man, his world-view and the wide influence he exercised on Sydney's intellectual society.

220 Liberality of opportunity: a history of Macquarie University 1964-1989.
Bruce Mansfield, Mark Hutchinson. Sydney: Macquarie University in association with Hale & Iremonger, 1992. 352p.

An academic history, commissioned by Sydney's Macquarie University as part of its celebration in 1992 of twenty-five years of teaching. Bruce Mansfield is a founding professor of the University, while Mark Hutchinson is an outsider and the book benefits from their differing perspectives on Macquarie, which was founded in response to an emergency in university enrolments in New South Wales.

221 The University of New South Wales: the Baxter years.
A. H. Willis.   Sydney: New South Wales University Press, 1983. 231p.

A history of the first twenty years of the life of the University of New South Wales, effectively the years when Professor Baxter was Vice-Chancellor (1949-69). It was originally called The New South Wales University of Technology, emphasizing its role in training scientific and technical manpower for the rapid industrial expansion of the post-war period. The author is Emeritus Professor of the University. He filled the Foundation Chair in Mechanical Engineering in 1956, became Pro-Vice-Chancellor in 1967 and retired from the University in 1978.

222 Technically and further: Sydney Technical College 1891-1991.
Norm Neill.   Sydney: Hale & Iremonger, 1991. 119p. bibliog.

Sydney Technical College is one of the world's largest educational institutions. Established in 1878 as the Working Men's College, it operated from rented premises before moving to the inner Sydney suburb of Ultimo in 1891. The book outlines the institution's beginnings and explores its varied history. However, it goes beyond the history of the College to review the evolution of technical and further education in New South Wales.

223 Sydney Teachers College: a history 1906-1981.
Graham Boardman and others.   Sydney: Hale & Iremonger, 1995. 253p. bibliog.

An academic history of Sydney Teachers College and the training of teachers for the school system in New South Wales. Another book on teacher training in New South Wales is *To enlighten them our task: a history of teacher education at Balmain and Kuring-gai Colleges 1946-1990,* by Cliff Turney and Judy Taylor (St Ives, New South Wales: Sydmac Academic Press, 1996. 208p.).

224 Ascham remembered 1886-1986.
Edited by Caroline Fairfax Simpson, Annette Fielding-Jones Dupree, Betty Winn Ferguson.   Sydney: The Fine Arts Press, 1986. 246p.

The centenary history of Ascham School, an exclusive private girl's school, situated in a Sydney harbourside suburb. The story is told by its Old Girls. Unlike state schools, most private schools to this day are segregated in Australia.

225 Shore: a history of Sydney Church of England Grammar School.
Geoffrey Sherrington.   Sydney: Sydney Church of England Grammar School in association with Allen & Unwin, 1983. 370p. bibliog.

Written by a professional historian, himself an old boy of the school, this is a cut above the usual school history, setting the school and its students in the wider community. Another book about the school was published by Peter Taylor, entitled *A celebration of*

Shore (Sydney: Sydney Church of England Grammar School in association with Allen & Unwin, 1988. 256p.). In the words of the author, it does not rival Sherrington's as a full history of the school, 'trying to capture its flavour rather than its fact'.

226 Grammar: a history of Sydney Grammar School 1819-1988.
Clifford Turney.   Sydney: Sydney Grammar School in association with Allen & Unwin, 1989. 490p. bibliog.

A history of a great, non-denominational private school established in 1854, written by the Professor of Education of the Faculty of Education at the University of Sydney. The focus of the book is on the development of the school 'within the broader, changing social contexts of city, state and nation which inevitably exerted an influence on what occurred in the School'. Sydney Grammar's Big School Room is the oldest secondary school building in Australia. It is the subject of a book by J. S. Sheldon, *The Big School Room at Sydney Grammar School with an account of the decline and fall of Sydney College* (Darlinghurst, New South Wales: Sydney Grammar School Press, 1997. 158p.).

Politics and Local
Government

**227 The advancement of local government in New South Wales 1906
to the present. Vol 3.**
F. A. Larcombe. Sydney: Sydney University Press in association
with Local Government Association of NSW and Shires Association
of NSW, 1978. 486p. bibliog.

This volume concludes the author's three-volume chronology, *A history of local
government in New South Wales*. The first volume, entitled *The origin of local
government in New South Wales 1831-1858*, was published in 1973 and the second, *The
stabilization of local government in New South Wales 1858-1906*, in 1976. Sydney's
various municipal authorities throughout the years are treated in great detail. The author
shows clearly that in the hierarchy of public administration, local government has always
been the poor relation, that it has had to be forced upon the community and that it has
rarely attracted men of great talent.

228 Sydney 1842-1992.
Shirley Fitzgerald. Sydney: Hale & Iremonger, 1992. 324p. plans.

This is the major volume in a Sydney History series being published to mark the
Sesquicentenary of the City of Sydney. Other volumes deal with municipalities in the
suburbs. This book documents some of the most important issues involved in the shaping
and managing of the city by the Sydney City Council. For anyone who wants to
understand Australia's foremost city today and the place of local government in the
Australian political structure, *Sydney 1842-1992* is required reading. The book is lavishly
illustrated.

**229 Sydney's electoral history: a short electoral history of Sydney
City Council 1842-1992.**
Hilary Golder. Sydney: Sydney City Council, 1995. 81p. maps.
tables.

This is the first work of any significance devoted primarily to an explanation and analysis
of the electoral basis of the Sydney City Council and the politics which resulted from that.

With the aid of maps the author shows the changing city boundaries and wards, variations in the franchise and the acts of Parliament regulating elections to the City Council. Party politics and the attempts to stack the council are also mentioned. There are illustrations of campaign posters. Renato Perdon's *Sydney's aldermen: a biographical register of Sydney City Aldermen 1842-1992* (Sydney: Sydney City Council, 1995. 117p.), is a companion volume.

230 Red hot: the life & times of Nick Origlass 1908-1996.
Hall Greenland. Sydney: Wellington Lane Press, 1998. 324p. bibliog.

This is as much the story of the Sydney suburb of Balmain, once a working-class area and home of radical politics in Sydney, now one of its most fashionable suburbs, as of its human subject. Origlass was a member of the Leichhardt Council for nearly thirty years and mayor from 1971 to 1973. He was an enthusiastic participant in radical politics all his life. He believed that it was the right of people, the rank and file, the residents, to determine their own destiny. He called this maximum democracy and for this belief he became the most expelled man in political history: from the Australian Labor Party and from various Communist parties and Trotskyite groupings. The author, a life-long disciple and associate of Origlass, has written a fascinating book about Sydney's local politics and one of its most colourful participants.

231 Change and challenge: a history of the municipality of Canterbury, N.S.W.
F. A. Larcombe. Sydney: Canterbury Municipal Council, 1979. 412p. maps. bibliog. tables.

The book deals with the history of the municipality of Canterbury with an emphasis on the development of the local council or local government. The author is an expert in his field and had previously published a major three-volume work, *A history of local government in New South Wales* (see item no. 227). In collaboration with W. B. Lynch he also co-authored a similar history of the municipality of Randwick, entitled *Randwick 1859-1976* (Sydney: Oswald Ziegler Publications for the Council of the Municipality of Randwick, 1976. 296p.).

232 Politics in a suburban community: the N.S.W. State elections in Manly, 1965.
Edited by John Power. Sydney: Sydney University Press, 1968. 194p. map. tables.

The 1965 New South Wales State elections brought to an end twenty-four years of continuous Labor Party rule in the State Parliament. This book is a study of the election campaign in a single electorate, the Sydney seaside electorate of Manly. In the Australian context, elections in the cities are usually fought out by the two main political parties: the Australian Labor Party and the Liberal-Country Party coalition. However, Manly has always been an atypical electorate in that, although demographically a Liberal electorate, it has over the years to this day tended to elect independent candidates. This book, resulting from a survey conducted by the Department of Government in the University of Sydney, provides an interesting insight into the Manly community, its politicians and its people.

233 Politics of the extreme Right: Warringah 1966.

R. W. Connell, Florence Gould.   Sydney: Sydney University Press, 1967. 115p. map. tables. (Sydney Studies in Politics, no. 7).

This study is concerned with the 1966 federal election in the Sydney suburban electorate of Warringah – the first campaign in which there was a serious challenge to established Australian political parties from the extreme Right and where right-wing elements tried to topple the Liberal candidate in a safe Liberal seat. It presents a detailed analysis of the campaign of the extreme Right movement and discusses the impact of extremism on the usual processes of local politics.

234 The secret army and the Premier: conservative paramilitary organisations in New South Wales 1930-32.

Andrew Moore.   Sydney: New South Wales University Press, 1989. 312p. bibliog.

A well-researched exposure of the efforts of the conservative forces to set up paramilitary organizations in New South Wales during the Great Depression to support the government against Communist subversion. The so-called 'Old Guard' was strongest in rural areas, but the brains and finances were located in Sydney and the inner core of the leadership of the movement reads like a who's who of Sydney society. On a higher level, Moore has documented the prevailing tendency of conservatives in 20th-century Australia to resort to planned subversion of State power when they do not control it.

Crime and Social Problems

235   Sydney in ferment: crime, dissent and official reaction 1788 to 1973.
Peter N. Grabosky.   Canberra: Australian National University Press, 1977. 205p. maps. bibliog. tables. graphs.

The author, a specialist in comparative criminology, describes and analyses trends in criminal behaviour, political dissidence, collective violence and crime control policies in Australia's oldest and largest metropolitan area over 185 years.

236   Drug traffic: narcotics and organized crime in Australia.
Alfred W. McCoy.   Sydney: Harper & Row, 1980. 455p. bibliog.

This was the first book dealing with organized crime in Australia, particularly Sydney, because its large population could support criminal activity, to treat the subject within an analytical framework. The author's training as a historian is reflected in the careful and detailed research. This research traces the growth of the vice trade, the illegal gambling trade, the penetration of licensed clubs by organized crime and the drug traffic through government reports, Royal Commissions and court transcripts. The emphasis throughout is on Sydney, where the majority of the inquiries have been held. The book is disturbing and interesting, as well as required reading for anyone interested in crime, drugs or politics.

237   The prince and the premier: the story of Perce Galea, Bob Askin and the others who gave organised crime its start in Australia.
David Hickie.   Sydney: Angus & Robertson, 1985. 536p.

Written by an investigative journalist, the book traces the history of modern organized crime in New South Wales, based in Sydney. The account begins with the gambling fraternity of the 1940s and 1950s, through its institutionalization during Sir Robert Askin's ten-year premiership of New South Wales (1965-75), to its emergence as a major political issue of the 1980s. It tells the inside story of corrupt politicians, crooked police, illegal casino bosses, sly-grog purveyors (people who sold alcohol illegally), vice profiteers and others who have played a part in organizing crime in Sydney and New South Wales.

238 The godfather in Australia: the book that started it all: organised crime's Australian connections.
Bob Bottom. Melbourne: Matchbooks, 1989. 202p.

A journalist's account of organized crime and mafia connections in Australia, much of it based in Sydney, as it is the largest city in Australia.

239 The Allens affair: how one man shook the foundations of a leading Australian law firm.
Valerie Lawson. Sydney: Macmillan, 1995. 291p. bibliog.

Adrian Powles reached the peak of the legal profession during the 1970s and 1980s as managing partner of the distinguished Sydney law firm of Allen Allen & Hemsley. No one knew that he was also a gambler at the track, the casino and in the financial marketplace. Valerie Lawson, an investigative journalist, here uncovers some fascinating facts behind the embezzlement scandal that nearly destroyed one of Australia's biggest and most secretive law firms.

240 Garden of evil: the granny killer's reign of terror.
Larry Writer with Steve Barrett, Simon Bouda. Sydney: Ironbark Press, 1992. 230p.

This is the story of Sydney's most notorious mass murderer, John Glover, who killed six elderly women in the suburbs of Sydney's North Shore. The book also provides an inside view of the police task force whose investigations under the intense community, political and media pressure finally led to the murderer. Another popular, journalistic account of the crime is Les Kennedy's and Mark Whittaker's *Granny killer: the story of John Glover* (Pymble, New South Wales: Collins/Angus & Robertson, 1992. 242p.).

241 Neddy: the life and crimes of Arthur Stanley Smith: an autobiography.
Arthur Stanley Smith, with Tom Noble. Sydney: Kerr, 1998. 2nd ed. 335p.

When this book by a notorious Sydney criminal was first published in 1993, it sparked current affairs shows, newspaper commentary and a television docu-drama entitled 'Blue murder'. Smith's confessions also triggered a massive inquiry into police corruption by the Independent Commission Against Corruption (ICAC), at which Smith appeared as a witness, while serving a life sentence in prison for murder and armed robbery. In 1995 he wrote another book entitled *Catch and kill your own: behind the killings the police don't want to investigate* (Sydney: Ironbark, 1995. 224p.), which deals with thirty-seven unsolved murders in Sydney. Both books are fascinating reads about Sydney's underworld, written with laconic, deadpan humour and a wonderful mastery of underground slang.

242   Chow Hayes: gunman.

David Hickie.   Sydney: Angus & Robertson, 1990. 368p.

The biography of the Sydney criminal Chow Hayes, who was involved in criminal activities from the 1920s to the 1970s. The book is based upon extensive interviews with Hayes with copious quotations of his own words. As well as telling the story of the king of Sydney's standover men (people who extorted money by intimidation), the book is in part a social history of crime in 20th-century Sydney. There are a number of photographs of notorious criminals. An appendix of eight pages lists Hayes' criminal record and convictions.

243   The shark arm murders: the thrilling true story of a tiger shark and a tattooed arm.

Alex Castles.   Adelaide: Wakefield Press, 1995. 182p.

In 1935 a Sydney aquarium shark coughed up a human arm, thus revealing one murder and precipitating another. The arm was forensically identified as belonging to a missing man named Jim Smith. A witness who could link an accused man to the killing of Smith was murdered before the trial took place. Subsequently, the accused was acquitted as Smith's body was never found. Fascination with the case has spawned several books and other writings, the present book being the latest. The author, Emeritus Professor of Law at the University of Adelaide, used newspapers, court transcripts, police archives and interviews for his book. He has structured it rather like a mystery novel, but also makes some useful and interesting observations about male attitudes in general and the attitudes of the police and the criminal underclasses in the Sydney of the 1930s in particular. It is aimed at the general reader.

244   Wild women of Sydney.

George Blaikie.   Adelaide: Rigby, 1980. 200p.

The author presents stories of three notorious women who ruled Sydney's underworld from the early 1930s to the mid-1940s. They were: Tilly Devine, 'Bordello Queen'; Kate Leigh, 'Sly Grog Queen'; and Nellie Cameron, 'Beauty Queen'. Between them, these three underworld queens had a total of 384 convictions for proven crimes.

245   Wild men of Sydney.

Cyril Pearl.   London: Allen, 1958. 255p.

This book deals with three remarkable rogues who bestrode the Sydney scene about the turn of the century. They were John Norton, William Willis and Paddy Crick, all of whom sat for many years as honourable members of the New South Wales Parliament. Their stories also mirror a forgotten town – the dirty, tough, intimate, turbulent, crooked, hard-drinking, politically immature Sydney of the late 19th century. A milder estimate of Norton's legacy is Michael Cannon's *That damned democrat: John Norton an Australian populist 1858-1916* (Carlton, Victoria: Melbourne University Press, 1981. 178p.). This book contains an extensive anthology of his journalism from the *Truth* newspaper, of which he was proprietor and editor until his death in 1916.

246   The Sydney assassins: a mid-Victorian mystery.

Leicester Cotton.   Melbourne: Lansdowne, 1964. 171p.

A reassessment of an unsolved double murder in Sydney in 1872, this book also presents a picture of life in Sydney during the 1870s.

247 Scallywags of Sydney Cove.
Frank Clune.   Sydney: Angus & Robertson, 1968. 182p.

A popular account of some of the more colourful and notorious criminals and political convicts who were transported to Sydney Cove from the arrival of the First Fleet in 1788 to the end of transportation in 1840. The book was republished in 1987 with the inclusion of many colour plates.

248 Sydney revels (the eighteen-fifties) of Bacchus, Cupid and Momus: being choice and humorous selections from scenes at the Sydney Police Office and other public places during the last three years.
Charles Adam Corbyn, presented by Cyril Pearl.   Sydney: Ure Smith, 1970. 103p.

A collection of police-court reports by Charles Adam Corbyn, who contributed these pieces to the *Empire* and *Bell's Life In Sydney* newspapers in the early 1850s. Here is a lusty picture of life in the Sydney of that time – a dirty, intimate, hard-drinking, evil-smelling town of no more than 75,000 people and no less than 400 public houses. Cyril Pearl introduces the book with a lengthy survey of the Sydney Corbyn lived in.

Business and Industry

249 Industrial awakening: a geography of Australian manufacturing, 1788-1890.
G. J. R. Linge. Canberra: Australian National University Press, 1979. 845p. maps. bibliog. tables. graphs.

The emphasis of the book is on the history of manufacturing industries in New South Wales and Victoria. Because of the concentration of population and its superior infrastructure, Sydney and its environs dominated the industrial scene in New South Wales and much of the text relates to the history of manufacturing in Sydney.

250 The Sydney markets 1788-1988.
Michael Christie. Sydney: Sydney Market Authority, 1988. 159p. bibliog.

This is a well-written and illustrated history of markets in Sydney from the time of white settlement in 1788 to 1988, the year of the Australian Bicentennial.

251 Shopkeepers and shoppers: a social history of retailing in New South Wales from 1788.
Frances Pollon. Sydney: The Retail Traders' Association of New South Wales, 1989. 382p. bibliog.

The introductory essay provides a good survey of many of the important developments in retail trading over 200 years. The major part of the book centres on Sydney and is organized by street and type of shop. The author concentrates on proprietors to the detriment of employees, customers and community. There are numerous well-produced and fascinating illustrations.

252 Gone to Gowings: a history of Gowing Bros.

Stephanie Gowing. Sydney: State Library of New South Wales Press, 1993. 96p. bibliog.

Gowing Bros is a Sydney institution. It is Australia's longest established family retailing firm. The story starts in 1868 when John Ellis Gowing advertised his 'new Mercery and Glove Depot' and takes us to 1993, when Gowing Bros was a company with a share portfolio worth $50 million. Thus the firm forms part of Sydney's social history. The book is copiously illustrated with black-and-white and colour photographs.

253 Cockatoo Island: Sydney's historic dockyard.

John Jeremy. Sydney: University of New South Wales Press, 1998. 263p.

A detailed history of Cockatoo Dockyard from its commencement in the 1850s on the largest island in Sydney Harbour, until its closure in 1991. For over a century it employed thousands of workers to build warships, remodel passenger liners, perform general ship repairs and later to modernize submarines. The text is supported by over 100 archival photographs and appendices listing ships built, refitted and repaired. The author, who spent thirty years of his working life on the island, was the last Chief Executive Officer of Cockatoo Dockyard.

254 First light: 150 years of gas.

Rosemary Broomham. Sydney: Hale & Iremonger, 1987. 240p. maps. bibliog. tables.

This publication marks the sesquicentenary of the establishment of the Australian Gas Light Company, which was charged by Act of Parliament 'to light with gas the town of Sydney in the colony of New South Wales...'. This is an interesting, richly illustrated history of a private company which has operated under its own name since 1837. It is one of Australia's oldest and most prominent businesses.

255 The grand parade: a history of the Royal Agricultural Society of New South Wales.

Brian H. Fletcher. Sydney: The Royal Agricultural Society of New South Wales, 1988. 328p. bibliog.

Easter in Sydney is traditionally associated with the agricultural show that has been held at Moore Park for well over a century. This book traces the history of the Royal Agricultural Society of New South Wales (RAS) which has conducted the show from its beginnings in 1822 to the present. The Royal Easter Show, as it is called, has become an outstanding event in the Australian calendar, a source of education and entertainment, where people from town and country are brought together to enjoy themselves and learn about one another's interests and occupations. There cannot be many Sydneysiders who, at some stage in their lives, have not enjoyed the agricultural exhibition, the competitions, such as wood-chopping, boxing, sheep shearing and horse-riding and the sideshow entertainment. The Show is recommended to the Easter-time visitor to Sydney. The book is richly illustrated.

256 Visions and profits: studies in the business career of Thomas Sutcliffe Mort.

Alan Barnard.   Melbourne: Melbourne University Press on behalf of the Australian National University, 1961. 234p.

An academic study of the business career of Thomas Sutcliffe Mort, Sydney's outstanding commercial personality of the mid-19th century. By the end of the 1840s he had built up a highly successful auctioneering business in Sydney and by the mid-1850s was not only a man of very considerable wealth, but was also acknowledged as the willing sponsor and promoter of endless worthy causes.

257 The respectable Sydney merchant: A. B. Spark of Tempe.

Graham Abbott, Geoffrey Little.   Sydney: Sydney University Press, 1976. 262p.

The book consists largely of the edited diaries of Alexander Brodie Spark (1792-1856), a Sydney merchant and businessman, who came to New South Wales in 1823 as a free settler. In Sydney in the booming 1820s and 1830s, Spark quickly established himself as a speculative trader who soon graduated to a rich banker and merchant, churchman, landowner and private collector. In colonial society he was a leading citizen and moved in the highest circles of the establishment. In 1844 he was declared bankrupt following the spectacular financial crashes of the early 1840s. The diaries span twenty years, 1836-56, and portray the commercial, political and social life of a brash, materialistic colonial society.

258 Samuel Terry: the Botany Bay Rothschild.

Gwyneth M. Dow.   Sydney: Sydney University Press, 1974. 266p. bibliog.

Samuel Terry (1776-1838) arrived in Sydney in 1801, having been transported for stealing 400 pairs of stockings. He died in 1838 as the richest man in New South Wales – in today's terms, a multi-millionaire, having left an estate of 250,000 pounds sterling and large property holdings in Sydney and the country. The author, a descendant of Terry, traces her ancestor's career in the business world of the early colony and describes the conflict which existed between the ex-convicts and those who came as free men. She shows the insurmountable social barriers of the day: although people of station, recognizing Terry's business acumen, associated with him in financial ventures, the Terrys were never invited to social occasions and Samuel Terry himself was denied directorships in business enterprises.

Economy and Finance

259 Economic growth of Australia, 1788-1821.
Edited by G. J. Abbott, N. B. Nairn.   Melbourne: Melbourne
University Press, 1969. 361p. maps. bibliog. tables. graphs.

As settlement had barely spread beyond the Sydney region by 1821 (except for Newcastle
and Tasmania), this economic history relates mainly to Sydney and its immediate
surroundings. The book consists of a collection of articles which trace the rudimentary
economic growth of the colony in the generation following the arrival of the European
settlers and convicts. The articles, written by academic specialists, provide an excellent
record of the struggling colony's early years.

**260 The bull, the bear and the kangaroo: the history of the Sydney
Stock Exchange.**
S. Salsbury, K. Sweeney.   Sydney: Allen & Unwin, 1988. 510p.

This is a comprehensive study of Australia's oldest and in many respects most important
stock exchange. It begins with the origins of share trading in New South Wales after 1817
and concludes with the merger of the Sydney exchange and its five state rivals into the
Australian Stock Exchange on April Fools Day, 1987. The same authors published a
companion volume, *Sydney stockbrokers: biographies of members of the Sydney Stock
Exchange 1871 to 1987* (Sydney: Hale & Iremonger, 1992. 466p.). This volume contains
the biographies of the 642 members of the Exchange for the period 1871-1987.

261 Fast forward: the history of the Sydney Futures Exchange.
Edna Carew.   Sydney: Allen & Unwin, 1993. 183p.

The Sydney Futures Exchange, founded in 1960 as the Sydney Greasy Wool Futures
Exchange, was the first outside the United States to trade in financial futures. During its
short history the SFE has evolved from a small institution focusing on wool to a global
force in financial futures and options, second only to the giant Japanese exchanges in the
Asia-Pacific region.

262 The Sydney traders: Simeon Lord and his contemporaries 1788-1821.
D. R. Hainsworth.   Melbourne: Melbourne University Press, 1981.
2nd ed. 264p. bibliog.

The author proves that, contrary to conventional belief, commercial enterprise flourished in the first forty years of settlement. This period was the social and economic seedtime of Australia, during which the foundations of Australian economic development were laid.

263 Sydney boom Sydney bust: the city and its property market 1850-1981.
M. T. Daly.   Sydney: Allen & Unwin, 1982. 227p. bibliog. tables.

This book, written by the Professor of Urban Geography at the University of Sydney, attempts to explain why the Sydney real estate market, both commercial and residential, is by far the most expensive in Australia.

264 Why cities change: urban development and economic change in Sydney.
Edited by Richard V. Cardew, John V. Langdale, David C. Rich.
Sydney: Allen & Unwin, 1982. 307p. maps. bibliog. tables.

This collection of articles by specialists examines certain aspects of economic change in Sydney during the 1970s. Topics discussed include office suburbanization, manufacturing and industrial property development, the wholesaling and retailing sectors, telecommunications, land-use, transport, the dimensions of urban unemployment and the role of finance and the capital market. The book has been written for the Geographical Society of New South Wales, which wanted to bring together research on Sydney's economic geography. It has been written with a specialist audience in mind.

265 Sydney Gay & Lesbian Mardi Gras: an evaluation of its economic impact.
Ian Marsh, John Greenfield.   Sydney: Sydney Gay & Lesbian
Mardi Gras Ltd, 1993. 89p. bibliog. tables.

Mardi Gras is a month-long celebration staged every February in Sydney, the parade attracting 500,000 spectators in 1993. It is one of the greatest gay and lesbian festivals in the world and attracts an increasing number of overseas visitors each year. This report presents an analysis of the festival's economic impact on Sydney.

Labour and
Employment

**266   All our labours: oral histories of working life in twentieth
century Sydney.**
Edited by John Shields.   Sydney: New South Wales University
Press, 1992. 252p. bibliog.

This volume consists of nine studies based on the oral testimonies of working people from
a range of occupations and workplaces. Their reflections are used by the contributing
authors to develop personal, lively and sometimes humorous, sometimes sobering
accounts of working life in Sydney between the First World War and the 1980s. Black-
and-white illustrations accompany the text.

267   The restless waterfront.
James Gaby.   Sydney: Antipodean Publishers, 1974. 252p.

The waterside workers or 'wharfies' always were and still are one of the most militant
workforces in Australia. In this book Captain James Gaby looks over the waterfront from
the point of view of a foreman, supervisor and manager of a stevedoring company, the
positions he held over a twenty-year period on the Sydney waterfront. The book is written
in an anecdotal, conversational style and contains some interesting photographs of work
on the wharves.

**268   With banner unfurled: the early years of the Ship Painters and
Dockers Union.**
Issy Wyner.   Sydney: Hale & Iremonger, 1983. 256p. bibliog.

This is a history of the formative years of the Union which grew into the New South
Wales Branch of the Federated Ship Painters and Dockers Union – a union of which the
author has been a member first as a rank-and-file painter and docker and then for over
thirty years as an elected official. The book also provides a look into the past of the
famous Sydney working-class suburb of Balmain – now gentrified – and the ship-
servicing industry which was born in the area.

269 Green bans, red union: environmental activism and the New South Wales Builders Labourers' Federation.
Meredith Burgmann, Verity Burgmann.   Sydney: UNSW Press, 1998. 352p. bibliog.

The authors have written a scholarly yet readable and interesting account of the radical unionism of builders labourers in New South Wales in the early 1970s. At the height of the building industry boom in the 1970s, a remarkable campaign stopped billions of dollars worth of indiscriminate development in Sydney, that was turning it into a concrete jungle. Enraging developers, employers and politicians, but delighting many in the community, the members of the New South Wales Builders Labourers Federation allied themselves with ordinary citizen activists to preserve Sydney's buildings, bush and parkland. The impact of the green bans movement can be seen all over Sydney today and long-lasting results were achieved through changes to environment and heritage legislation and the philosophy of town planning. At the time such worker environmental protest was unique and attracted world-wide attention.

270 Sydney's burning.
Ian Turner.   London: Heinemann, 1969. rev. ed. 254p. bibliog.

This book is the first full-scale study of the trial in Sydney for seditious conspiracy during the First World War of twelve men who were members or alleged members of the revolutionary organization known as the Industrial Workers of the World, or IWW, which originated in the United States. Following the arrest of one of the men for sedition, a series of fires broke out in Sydney and the twelve men were tried and convicted for arson and sentenced to long terms of imprisonment. However, after the war in less hysterical circumstances all were released from prison by the end of 1921 because of insufficient evidence of their guilt.

271 Servant and master: building and running the grand houses of Sydney 1788-1850.
Barrie Dyster.   Sydney: NSWU Press, 1989. 189p. bibliog.

The Historic Houses Trust of New South Wales conceived the idea of this book in order to research and thereby gain a better appreciation of the role of servants and tradesmen in colonial society. The focus was on the people who built and maintained colonial houses in Sydney. The author is an economic historian with extensive knowledge of 19th-century labour history. The book is based on unique documents, many reproduced in the book, which reveal not only social and commercial relationships, aesthetic concerns and worries about workmanship, but also more mundane information about the price of bricks or the daily rates for carpenters. There are also many magnificent reproductions of artworks, depicting the houses under discussion.

272 These outcast women: the Parramatta Female Factory 1821-1848.
Annette Salt.   Sydney: Hale & Iremonger, 1984. 160p. bibliog.

The female factory at Parramatta was ostensibly a place to house and employ female convicts on their arrival in the colony of New South Wales. In this study of the institution, the author, a historian, examines the many-sided role it played in the lives of early Australian women – employment bureau, marriage bureau, maternity ward, prison and refuge. She also traces the founding of the factory, the changing ideals about its purpose, the administrative problems it faced, and its failure to become economically viable. Sadly, the book does not tell the reader much about the women themselves.

Transport

273 Getting around town: a history of urban transport in Australia.
Brian Carroll.   Sydney: Cassell, 1980. 176p.

A popular history of urban transport in Australia. The text is supported with many
contemporary illustrations. Horses and carts, steam and electric trains, trams powered by
horses, steam, cables and electricity, ferries, cars, taxis, buses and bicycles are all
discussed in detail and there is also information on bridges, transport strikes and petrol
rationing. Sydney is mentioned throughout the book and specific chapters are devoted to
its transport modes and traffic problems.

274 Sydney's transport: studies in urban history.
Edited by Garry Wotherspoon.   Sydney: Hale & Iremonger in
association with Sydney History Group, 1983. 212p. maps. bibliog.
diagrams. tables.

This book is the third collection of essays by the Sydney History Group, which was
formed in 1975 to foster interest in the city's history. The scope of the volume is wide. It
covers virtually the complete period of white settlement and deals with most modes of
transport: shipping, ferries, horse buses and wagons, tramways (horse drawn, steam and
electric), trains, omnibuses, cars and even – though in passing – the bicycle. This is the
first comprehensive collection of essays to deal with the city and its transport in an
analytic way. The essays have been written with accessibility to a wider public in mind.

**275 Juggernaut: a story of Sydney in the wild days of the steam
trams.**
David Burke.   Sydney: Kangaroo Press, 1997. 152p. bibliog.

Steam trams, popularly known as 'Juggernauts', began service in Sydney in 1879. Until
they were supplanted by electrically powered trams in the early 1900s, the juggernauts
recorded more than sixty million passenger journeys each year. Sydney operated the
world's largest steam tram network. This delightful book, packed with reproductions of
contemporary documents, photographs and caricatures, tells the story of this form of
transport in late 19th-century Sydney.

276   From city to suburb … a fifty year journey (The story of N.S.W. government buses).
Greg Travers.   Sydney: The Sydney Tramway Museum, 1982.
228p. maps.

This book commemorates the inauguration of Government operated bus services on Christmas Day 1932 and traces the subsequent development of services in Sydney and Newcastle during the next fifty years to 1982. The text is packed with detail and is especially valuable for the hundreds of photographs depicting the various types of buses used throughout the fifty-year period. There is no index or bibliography. Travers also wrote *A brief pictorial history of the government bus* (Sydney: Historic Commercial Vehicle Association Co-op, 1990. 84p.).

277   Making the railways.
David Burke.   Sydney: State Library of New South Wales Press in association with the State Rail Authority of NSW, 1995. 262p.

The first railway journey in Australia took place in 1855, when a train made the trip from Sydney to Parramatta – a distance of 22 kilometres. This book presents a history of the state railways of New South Wales and Sydney. It is illustrated with many black-and-white photographs and the text is enhanced by oral history interviews with staff working for the state railways at various levels of responsibility. There is no bibliography, but each chapter has end-notes which include sources consulted.

278   Railway relics and romance: the Eveleigh Railway Workshops, Sydney, New South Wales.
Photographed by David Moore.   Sydney: Caroline Simpson, 1996.
120p.

The Eveleigh Railway Workshops, situated in the inner suburb of Redfern, were built from 1887 to service the great era of steam locomotives and railway expansion in New South Wales. By 1925 some 153 locomotives had been built and the Workshops reached their zenith during the 1950s when they employed over 5,000 workers. Eveleigh closed in 1988, a victim of the transition from steam to diesel electric powered locomotives. In this large-format volume, professional photographer David Moore evokes with his artistic images the heritage of the Workshops. The accompanying text pays tribute to the men who worked there.

279   Ferries of Sydney.
Graeme Andrews.   Sydney: Sydney University Press in association with Oxford University Press, 1994. 3rd ed. 264p. bibliog.

Sydney Harbour ferry service is Australia's first and oldest continual public transport system. This new edition offers a major expansion and revision of the history of the Sydney ferries. Many new illustrations have also been included. *Manly ferries of Sydney Harbour* by Tom Mead (Sydney: Dolphin Books, 1994. rev. ed. 187p.), is a copiously illustrated history of the ferry service from Sydney city to Manly, an oceanside suburb.

280 Seaport gateways of Australia.
James Bird. London: Oxford University Press, 1968. 253p. bibliogs.

Essentially a brief, readable history of the development of the major ports in Australia, starting with some interesting comparisons of the original reasons for selecting each site. The ports discussed include Sydney with Botany Bay, followed by ports in other states.

281 A century of ships in Sydney Harbour.
Ross Gillett, Michael Melliar-Phelps. Adelaide: Rigby, 1980. 160p.

This popular, pictorial work contains over 200 photographs of every type of vessel that has frequented Sydney Harbour. The illustrations range from sailing ships to passenger liners and include tugs, ferries, cargo carrying ships, fireboats, warships, pilot boats, container ships and many others. It is a book for the shipping enthusiast.

282 Shipping arrivals and departures, Sydney, Volume 3, 1841-1844 and gazetteer.
Graeme Broxam, Ian Nicholson. Canberra: Roebuck Books, 1988. 324p. 159p. maps. (Roebuck Society Publication, no. 34).

The primary objective of this listing is to provide a record of shipping movements in and out of the port of Sydney from 1 January 1841 to 31 December 1844. This follows on from the initial volume: *Shipping arrivals and departures, Sydney, 1788-1825* by J. S. Cumpston (Canberra: Roebuck Society, 1977); and *Shipping arrivals and departures. Volume 2 1826-1840 Parts I, II and III* by Ian Hawkins Nicholson ([Canberra]: Roebuck Society, 1977). *Gazetteer of Sydney shipping 1788-1840,* also by Nicholson (Canberra: Roebuck Society, 1981. 217p.), is a geographical index of ports of origin and destination and places discovered, visited or remarked upon by Sydney shipping of the period. The *Gazetteer* is in effect an index of place-names for the previous three volumes. This last volume is illustrated and contains numerous maps, charts and plans.

283 From bullocks to Boeings: an illustrated history of Sydney Airport.
Jennifer Gall. Canberra: Australian Government Publishing Service, 1986. 76p. maps. bibliog.

This book traces the history of Sydney Kingsford Smith Airport, from its 'bullock paddock' origins to a bustling centre of aviation industry activity. By far the busiest airport in Australia, it is also ideally located, being in the centre of Sydney's industrial heartland and only eight kilometres away from the city's Central Business District. The proximity of a huge residential population has always created problems of expansion of the airport and with aircraft noise, vibration, pollution and interference with radio and television reception. Efforts to shift Sydney's major airport outside the city limits have to this day proved fruitless.

284 The Sydney airport fiasco: the politics of an environmental nightmare.
Paul Fitzgerald. Sydney: Hale & Iremonger, 1998. 250p. bibliog.

According to the author, the fifty-year history of Sydney's Kingsford Smith Airport is the history of an environmental disaster. Surrounded by residential areas on a site only one-third the size of any comparable airport, with inefficient split terminals, it degrades the living conditions of hundreds of thousands of Sydney's residents. The author argues that the building of the Airport's third runway, which opened in 1995, was not a decision which was based on safety considerations, effectiveness, or environmental sustainability. It was a political decision upholding the interests of the airline industry and big business, which ignored the public interest and welfare.

Environment

285 Out of sight: Sydney's environmental history, 1851-1981.
Dan Coward.   Canberra: Department of Economic History,
Australian National University, 1988. 328p. maps. bibliog. tables.

The main theme of this book is an exploration of the origins and development of public
health policy in Sydney during the 19th century and its evolution into an explicit
environmental management policy during the 1960s and 1970s. Although arising from
research conducted at the Institute of Advanced Studies at the Australian National
University in Canberra, the text is suited to the lay reader.

**286 Toxic fish and sewer surfing: how deceit and collusion are
destroying our great beaches.**
Sharon Beder.   Sydney: Allen & Unwin, 1989. 176p. maps. bibliog.
tables.

Sydney and its suburbs are blessed with magnificent beaches. Pollution, however, is an
ever-present hazard. Millions of litres of nearly raw sewage, mixed with toxic industrial
waste, are pumped out into the ocean daily. Sharon Beder, a lecturer at the University of
New South Wales, examines the problem in great detail and puts much of the blame on
the Sydney sewerage and water authorities. The book is packed with graphic material
such as maps and graphs and good use is made of telling cartoons about the problem.

287 Greenprint for Sydney.
Edited by Jeff Angel.   Sydney: Total Environment Centre, 1999.
102p. maps.

Total Environment Centre (TEC) is a non-profit, non-government organization
established in 1972 as an environmental advocacy centre. Since then it has worked on a
wide range of environmental protection campaigns – natural and urban, coastal and
inland, country and city. Starting with the premise that Sydney is in an environmental
crisis, twenty-one specialists in the environmental movement have prepared concise
papers to identify the main problems and the agenda for Sydney's future development.

288 Green bans: the birth of Australian environmental politics, a study in public opinion and participation.
Richard J. Roddewig. Sydney: Hale & Iremonger with the Conservation Foundation (Washington), 1978. 180p.

The more obviously political actions of Australian trade unions in the 1970s involved strikes or bans against the export of merino sheep, uranium mining, tours of sporting teams from South Africa and the demolition of historic or otherwise significant buildings, the latter leading to the celebrated green bans in Sydney. Australian law at that time made public participation in the protection of the natural and built environment almost impossible as development reigned supreme. With no help from the law, the alternative was direct action. When the militant Builders Labourers Federation put in place its green bans to protect the interests of the Sydney middle class, it was an event unique to Australia. Roddewig, an American land use attorney who visited Australia to study this novel phenomenon, has written a lucid, perceptive text, which owes much to his experience in a very different legal tradition and the author's comparative approach.

289 Green bans & beyond.
Jack Mundey. Sydney: Angus & Robertson, 1981. 154p.

This is the autobiography of Jack Mundey, life-long trade unionist and Secretary of the New South Wales Branch of the Builders Labourers Federation during the early 1970s, when the union achieved world-wide fame for its 'green bans' policy. The policy had its roots in environmental protection. From the first green ban in 1971, which was to prevent the bulldozing of an area of greenery – Kelly's Bush – near Sydney Harbour, to three years later, approximately fifty green bans had stopped an estimated $4000 million in construction projects in Sydney on parkland, historic areas of the city and low-cost residential areas. Mundey tells the story of these struggles and sets out his ideas about citizen participation in environmental protection. Patrick White, Australia's Nobel Prize winner for Literature in his book *Flaws in the glass,* refers to Jack Mundey as 'dedicated conservationist, idealist alas, and for me one of the most impressive Australians'.

290 The history of the battle to save Kelly's Bush and the green ban movement in the early 1970s.
Margaret Shaw. Sydney: Buckleys Publications, 1996. 67p. bibliog.

An account of the environmental battle to save a wilderness area on Sydney Harbour, close to the Central Business District, written by one of the participants. The campaign led to an historic alliance between the middle-class women, who started the fight, and the militant Builders Labourers Federation, which resulted in the union placing a green ban on a housing development on the site of Kelly's Bush. Eventually, green bans were placed on many multi-million dollar development projects across Sydney in historically and environmentally sensitive areas. Pip Kalajzich published an illustrated booklet entitled *The battlers for Kelly's Bush* ([Sydney]: Battlers for Kelly's Bush, 1996. 84p.). Here ten of the thirteen women who formed the original 'battlers' group tell their stories of the protest.

291   A river revived: the Parramatta.

Carol Powell.   Sydney: New South Wales University Press, 1987. 102p. maps. bibliog.

The Parramatta river is a large tidal estuary of Sydney Harbour. It starts at Parramatta, the second settlement in Australia after Sydney. Because of the difficult land terrain, the River has always formed an important transport link. As industries arose along its shores, effluents and official neglect led to heavy pollution of its waters, a common problem of Sydney's waterways. This richly illustrated book is a history of the river and the efforts to save it from environmental degradation. It also takes the reader on a guided tour of the waterway, recalling the past and recounting historical highlights along the way.

292   Losing ground: an environmental history of the Hawkesbury–Nepean catchment.

Sue Rosen.   Sydney: Hale & Iremonger, 1995. 190p. maps. bibliog.

This book traces the history of land use and environmental change in the Hawkesbury–Nepean River system and its catchment area. The system is vitally important for the Sydney region as it supplies most of its water requirements. The author presents a pessimistic picture of the current state of the river system. Signs of stress include algal blooms, water discolouration, changed temperature patterns, odours and the displacement of native flora and fauna. The work began as a technical study on the impact of European land use on the catchment area, commissioned by the Sydney Water Board. Rosen has skilfully turned it into a very accessible work of history.

Architecture and Urban Planning

General architecture

293 Sydney architecture.
John Haskell, photographs by John Callanan.   Sydney: UNSW
Press, 1997. 96p.

The author, an academic architect and popularizer of architecture in articles in the *Sydney Morning Herald,* presents here some of Sydney's finest and most interesting architecture. Intended as a walking guide, the book is divided into five sections, each covering a particular part of the city and suburbs. Superb photographs and delightful sketches of buildings and vistas accompany the text. The author has also written *Haskell's Sydney* (Sydney: Hale & Iremonger, 1983. 200p.), which principally contains articles he first published in the *Sydney Morning Herald.* Written in accessible language, they are a very good introduction to Sydney's architecture for the layman.

294 Sydney architecture.
Graham Jahn.   Sydney: Watermark Press, 1997. 256p. maps. plans.

The book lists more than 500 buildings from early colonial dwellings to the modern architecture of today. It provides detailed historical, architectural and sometimes anecdotal notes and brief biographies of leading architects. The text is supported by original photographs, as well as house plans and location maps for suggested tours. It is an excellent guide to the architectural history of Sydney for both visitor and resident. The author is a well-known Sydney architect, who is also a Councillor of the City of Sydney and chairman of its Planning Committee.

295 Sydney: a guide to recent architecture.
Francesca Morrison.   London: Ellipsis Konemann, 1997. 316p.

This guide introduces more than 100 buildings and urban projects – from major public and commercial buildings to small housing conversions and restaurants – completed in the Sydney metropolitan area since 1985. It aims to give an understanding of the state of architecture in the city and to reveal something of Sydney's culture and the concerns of its citizens. The guide is divided into six sections which cover the various geographical areas of Sydney where there are buildings of interest. Every building is photographed and there is a detailed description about its history, purpose and architectural features. It is a perfect guidebook for those architecturally inclined, as its format is small enough to fit the pocket.

296 Shaping Sydney: a public architecture & civic decorum.
Chris Johnson. Sydney: Hale & Iremonger, 1999. 240p. bibliog.

A lavishly illustrated history by the current New South Wales Government Architect about the work, often controversial, of colonial and state government architects. The period covered is from the era of Francis Greenway in the 1810s to the present.

297 Old Sydney buildings: a social history.
Margaret Simpson. Sydney: Kangaroo Press, 1995. 196p. bibliog.

The book aims to provide the full history of Sydney's old buildings within a five-kilometre radius of the Sydney General Post Office. The author pays a lot of attention to the people, institutions and companies which have used the buildings, the changing functions they have had over time and the story behind their survival and restoration. In short, the book provides an insight into Sydney's social, cultural, industrial and institutional life through its re-used, old buildings. Every building discussed is illustrated by drawings, photographs and plans.

298 Sydney as it might have been: dreams that died on the drawing board.
Eric Irving. Sydney: Alpha Books, 1974. 157p. bibliog.

This book outlines the history of grandiose plans of buildings and other structures proposed for Sydney, but for various reasons never built. The book contains eighty illustrations, most of them copies of original sketches or working plans with a text to unite them into a continuing story from the city's earliest days. As well as the familiar reasons the author advances for the non-realization of the projects, such as lack of money, political infighting and power struggles, he offers others, such as mere inactivity and the lapse of time. This is a fascinating look at Sydney as it might have been.

299 The early Australian architects and their work.
Morton Herman. Sydney: Angus & Robertson, 1970. 2nd ed. 248p. bibliog.

A pioneering work by a professional architect based on long and careful research, which presents a detailed account of colonial buildings in Sydney (with some asides to the rest of New South Wales) from 1788 to 1845. 127 careful scale drawings, some in colour, by the author, support the informative text, which also brings to life the many builders and architects of the period. This book first appeared in 1954, and in 1956 Herman wrote *The architecture of Victorian Sydney* (Sydney: Angus & Robertson, 1964. 2nd ed. 192p.), which takes the story of Sydney's architecture from 1850 to 1901. The story is told mostly in 40 drawings by the author and 242 photographs, with minimal text.

300 **Foundations of identity: building early Sydney 1788-1822.**
Peter Bridges.   Sydney: Hale & Iremonger, 1995. 186p. maps.
bibliog.

The central theme of this book is the building and shaping of Sydney from the time of the arrival of the First Fleet in January 1788, to the departure of Governor Macquarie in February 1822. While dealing mainly with the physical evolution of the settlement, the book does not neglect the problems which the pioneer settlers faced in establishing themselves in a new land. The author was formerly an architect in the New South Wales Public Works Department, where he headed a group established to care for historic buildings. He writes in an accessible style and with a wry humour. The work is an ideal companion for seeing Sydney. It is illustrated with contemporary pictures.

301 **Fine houses of Sydney.**
Robert Irving, John Kinstler, Max Dupain.   Sydney: Methuen,
1982. 197p. bibliog.

A lavishly produced book describing in text and pictures twenty-one distinctive examples of Sydney's domestic architecture, dating from the early 19th century to the present. The range of architectural styles is quite astonishing. The excellent photography of the buildings and their interiors contributes much to the success of this folio-size volume.

302 **Early colonial houses of New South Wales.**
Rachel Roxburgh, photographs by Douglas Baglin.   Sydney:
Lansdowne Press, 1974. 603p. bibliog.

A loving, detailed study of some fifty houses dating from the early years of settlement. Sixteen houses in the Sydney region are covered in the first third of the book, which is lavishly illustrated with photographs and drawings. It is a mine of information not only on the houses, but also on the intimate personal history of the owners.

303 **Early colonial homes of the Sydney region 1788-1838.**
Daphne Kingston.   Sydney: Kangaroo Press, 1990. 96p. bibliog.

The drawings in this large-format volume cover the Sydney metropolitan area and extend in a circle bounded by Wiseman's Ferry, Wilberforce, Wallacia, Camden, Campbelltown and Appin. The brief text accompanying each drawing has been selected to describe life during the early days of each house and its later fortunes. Kingston, a trained artist, has written two earlier books on Sydney's old buildings: *Early slab buildings of the Sydney region* (Kenthurst, New South Wales: Kangaroo Press, 1985. 119p.); and *Sydney's hidden charms* (Kenthurst, New South Wales: Kangaroo Press, 1987. 119p.). They also feature drawings by the author of domestic architecture of the 19th century.

304 **Demolished houses of Sydney.**
Edited by Joy Hughes.   Sydney: Historic Houses Trust of New
South Wales, 1999. 144p.

This book is the catalogue for a Historic Houses exhibition at the Hyde Park Barracks in Sydney. Together with photographs and sketches for each house, it lists Sydney's houses – ranging from humble to grand – which were built between 1788 and 1968 and demolished from 1845 to 1998. Introductory essays discuss and evaluate whether

Architecture and Urban Planning. Urban planning, engineering and infrastructure

Sydney's architectural heritage has suffered from the demolitions. The book is arranged by geographical area.

305   The architectural character of Glebe Sydney.
Bernard Smith, Kate Smith.   Sydney: University Co-operative Bookshop, 1973. 128p. bibliog.

The Glebe is an inner city area of Sydney next to the Central Business District, which presents a microcosm of late colonial domestic architecture with a small extension into what is called Federation style. The houses have escaped demolition and are now being preserved. The book presents 214 pictures of buildings in chronological order, so that the reader can follow the development in style that occurred. Bernard Smith is one of Australia's best known art critics and historians and this book led to a better appreciation of the beauty of all inner suburbs of the large Australian cities.

306   Sydney in 1848: a facsimile of the original text and copper-plate engravings of its principal streets, public buildings, churches, chapels, etc., from drawings.
Joseph Fowles.   Sydney: Ure Smith in association with the National Trust of Australia (NSW), 1973. 104p.

Joseph Fowles, an English marine artist, came to Sydney in 1838 and in 1848 published a remarkable pictorial album of what he called the 'flourishing metropolis of Australasia' – Sydney. The book is now republished in a facsimile edition from engravings of the original text and plates, with a foreword by architectural historian Morton Herman, and with an index and many annotations. The book is an accurate representation of Sydney as it appeared in the mid-19th century and is a true architectural record of the buildings lining Sydney's important thoroughfares. Fowles also alludes to Sydney's history and the social life of the times.

Urban planning, engineering and infrastructure

307   Living for the city: urban Australia crisis or challenge.
Tony Collins.   Sydney: ABC Books for the Australian Broadcasting Corporation, 1993. 158p.

A look at the main present-day problem in Australian cities: the unplanned urban sprawl. The author suggests future changes based on environmental and humanist considerations. The discussion covers the whole country, drawing many examples from Sydney's problems and its attempted solutions to urban planning and development.

Architecture and Urban Planning. Urban planning, engineering and infrastructure

308   Property, politics and urban planning: a history of Australian city planning 1890-1990.
Leonie Sandercock.   New Brunswick, New Jersey: Transaction Publishers, 1990. 2nd ed. 302p. bibliog.

A study of the development of town planning in Adelaide, Melbourne and Sydney. Originally published in 1977 as *Cities for sale: property, politics and urban planning in Australia,* this second edition retains the text of the earlier edition, but includes a new thirty-six page introduction which updates the narrative chronologically. The author also reflects self-critically on her methodology and theory in the light of debates in this field since the mid-1970s.

309   Planning Sydney's future.
Peter Spearritt, Christina De Marco.   Sydney: Allen & Unwin in conjunction with the Department of Planning, New South Wales, 1988. 150p. maps. bibliog. tables. diagrams.

This book is a companion volume to the report on metropolitan strategy published by the New South Wales government under the title *Sydney into its third century* (Sydney: Department of Planning, 1988. 72p.). It is a breezy account of the history, present and future of urban planning in Sydney, mixed with a great variety of maps, photographs, cartoons, models, tables, advertisements, brochures and sketches. Seldom have urban plans been put into such an interesting format. All the great plans for Sydney – 1909, 1948, 1968 and 1988 – are set in their context and discussed at length. Altogether, this is an accessible view of Sydney's planning history for the layman.

310   The accidental city: planning Sydney since 1788.
Paul Ashton.   Sydney: Hale & Iremonger, 1995. 128p. maps. bibliog.

This book is not about the metropolis of Sydney and its sprawling suburbs, but is limited in scope to the area controlled by the Sydney City Council, which includes the Central Business District and the inner suburbs. It is also mainly concerned with the politics of planning and building, focusing on the City Council's role. The author demonstrates effectively that the Sydney municipal authorities have rarely tried to exercise strict control, generally preferring a laissez-faire approach, which favours the few – the developers and speculators – at the expense of the majority – the citizens of the city. The book is richly illustrated with photographs, plans and diagrams, which are well integrated with the text. The Council of the City of Sydney has also published *Planning Sydney: nine planners remember* (Sydney: Council of the City of Sydney, 1992. 203p.), containing interviews conducted by Paul Ashton and aides, which were used as raw material for *The accidental city.*

311   The design of Sydney: three decades of change in the city centre.
Edited by G. P. Webber.   Sydney: Law Book Company, 1988. 220p. maps.

The book consists of essays on planning and projects carried out in Sydney's Central Business District. The essays are of special importance because they have been written by the people whose efforts have helped to shape the city's physical form. The nine contributors – urban planners, architects and historians – have been intimately involved

Architecture and Urban Planning. Urban planning, engineering and infrastructure

in, and in several cases, been in charge of, the planning, designing and building of the physical environment of the city. The text is greatly enhanced by the hundreds of illustrations, which include photographs, sketches, plans and designs.

312 Sydney's great experiment: the progress of the Cumberland County Plan.
Denis Winston.   Sydney: Angus & Robertson, 1957. 146p. maps. bibliog.

This is an exposition of the first of the post-Second World War urban plans for Sydney. The book aims to describe the planning scheme and its main objectives, the reasons for the latter, the methods used to achieve them and the progress made so far. In conclusion, the advantages and disadvantages of the plan are weighed up and future prospects estimated. The book is illustrated by ten maps and diagrams in colour and twenty-two full-page photographs. The appendices include extracts from the relevant Local Government Act and the Scheme Ordinance.

313 Sydney from settlement to city: an engineering history of Sydney.
Edited by Don Fraser.   Sydney: Engineers Australia, 1989. 328p. maps.

A cooperative venture by the Engineering Heritage Committee of the Sydney Division of the Institution of Engineers Australia for the Australian Bicentennial Celebrations in 1988. The Committee co-opted twenty expert authors, who wrote chapters for this handsome, large-format book, telling the story of public engineering developments in Sydney over 200 years. It is written in an accessible style, and the expert as well as the general reader will enjoy this history, not least for its hundreds of informative photographs and drawings. Sadly, no bibliography is provided.

314 The unreasonable man: the life and works of J. J. C. Bradfield.
Richard Raxworthy.   Sydney: Hale & Iremonger, 1989. 153p. maps. bibliog.

After graduating brilliantly in engineering from Sydney University in 1889, Bradfield went on to a life-long career in the New South Wales Public Works Department. During his long life Bradfield designed bridges, roads, dams, railways and tramways, but he is best known for his work on the Sydney Harbour Bridge, which opened in 1932. This well-illustrated book is a tribute to an engineer who achieved an international reputation and was responsible for much of Sydney's engineering infrastructure during his forty years at the Public Works Department.

315 Sydney tunnels.
Brian Kennedy, Barbara Kennedy.   Sydney: Kangaroo Press, 1993. 96p. maps.

Under the streets of Sydney lies a network of tunnels that spreads for tens of kilometres. Many of these underground ways carry the essential services vital to a city of nearly four million people, but there are also a surprising number that have been used, or are still being used, for such purposes as mining and defence. This book presents a comprehensive survey of all the tunnels dug beneath the city – from Sydney's first water supply tunnel, dug not long after the first European settlement, to the recently constructed Sydney Harbour Tunnel, which relieves the Sydney Harbour Bridge of some of its traffic pressure.

316 Fifty years of electricity supply: the story of Sydney's Electricity Undertaking.

Gordon F. Anderson. Sydney: The Sydney County Council, 1955. 257p.

The 8 July 1954 marked the fiftieth anniversary of the inauguration of the public supply of electricity in the City of Sydney. This book celebrates the historic fiftieth anniversary. It presents the story of the Sydney Electricity Undertaking, the body charged with the responsibility of supplying electrical power to the Sydney metropolitan area. The text is based on the official records of the Electricity Undertaking.

317 The sweat of their brows: 100 years of the Sydney Water Board 1888-1988.

Margo Beasley. Sydney: Water Board, Sydney, Illawarra, Blue Mountains, 1988. 223p. maps.

An account of the development and history of the water supply, sewerage and drainage systems of Sydney from their beginnings with the first settlement in 1788 to 1988, after their control was vested in a Board specifically constituted for the purpose. Two previous official histories of the Board have been published: *The water supply and sewerage of Sydney*, by F. J. J. Henry in 1939 and *The water supply sewerage and drainage of Sydney*, by W. V. Aird in 1961. The present book tells a more informal story which underlies the Board's achievements. It takes a human, behind-the-scenes look at a complex institution and includes humorous and revealing reminiscences from many of the people who actually built the structures. Hundreds of dramatic photographs from the Board's own collection serve as illustrations.

318 Fighting fire! A century of service 1884-1984.

Colin Adrian. Sydney: Allen & Unwin, 1984. 271p. bibliog. tables.

In its centenary year, 1984, the Sydney fire service included seventy-three fire stations staffed by more than 2000 firefighters. In this thoroughly researched history, the author shows the growth of the fire service from its humble beginnings, to become, by 1984, the largest autonomous fire fighting organization in the western world with an annual expenditure in excess of $100 million. The book is profusely illustrated with cartoons and photographs, many of a dramatic nature.

Specific features

319 Opera House: act one.
David Messent. Sydney: David Messent Photography, 1997. 544p. bibliog. plans.

Since the Sydney Opera House was opened in 1973, its sail-like roof covered in white ceramic tiles suggestive of the yachts that sail on Sydney Harbour has become a symbol of Sydney, like the Harbour Bridge which towers over it. This book presents a thorough narrative history of the spectacular building from the time of the international competition for its design, won by Danish architect Jorn Utzon, through the controversies of the changes in the building design during the construction process to its completion. The book is based on private papers, interviews and previous written material and is full of interesting detail and anecdote. There are sixty-seven illustrations of the building process and plans. Extensive references complete the text.

320 Sydney Opera House: Jorn Utzon.
Phillip Drew. London: Phaidon Press, 1995. 60p. bibliog. plans. (Architecture in Detail).

This large-format, illustrated book is published in the series Architecture in Detail, a series of superbly photographed and technically informative monographs, which embraces a wide range of internationally renowned buildings. This book outlines the design concept and construction of the Sydney Opera House and contains a comprehensive set of technical drawings and working details, a bibliography and chronology of the building. In a sense, it is the definitive work on the subject, intended for architecture enthusiasts, practitioners and students alike. A more voluminous book treating the subject on similar lines is Vincent Smith's *The Sydney Opera House* (Sydney: Summit Books, 1974. 160p.).

321 The masterpiece: Jorn Utzon: a secret life.
Phillip Drew. Melbourne: Hardie Grant Books, 1999. 574p. bibliog.

Although its architect Jorn Utzon did not supervise the construction of his masterpiece, the Sydney Opera House, to the end for political reasons beyond his control, the completed Opera House is considered one of the world's great architectural wonders. This book is a dual biography: of the design and construction of the Opera House and of its enigmatic architect. Phillip Drew, an internationally renowned architectural writer, also introduces other brilliant, but less well-known, of Utzon's works.

322 The Sydney Harbour Bridge.
Peter Spearritt. Sydney: Allen & Unwin, 1982. 120p. bibliog.

When it opened on 19 March 1932, in the middle of the Great Depression, the Sydney Harbour Bridge was the largest arch bridge in the world and changed the shape of Sydney forever. Today the 'coathanger' has been joined by another Sydney symbol – the Opera House, built in its shadow. This book celebrates the fiftieth anniversary of the Harbour Bridge, detailing its history in text and hundreds of historic illustrations of its construction phases, in photographs and cartoons and as an icon on stamps, tourist publications and in art. In 1982 a similar book appeared by David Ellyard and Richard Raxworthy, *The proud arch: the story of the Sydney Harbour Bridge* (Sydney: Bay Books, 1982. 160p.).

323 The Sydney Harbour Bridge 1932-1982: a golden anniversary celebration.
Ursula Prunster. Sydney: Angus & Robertson in association with Art Gallery of New South Wales, 1982. 134p.

For the fiftieth anniversary of the completion of the Sydney Harbour Bridge, the Art Gallery of New South Wales mounted an exhibition to celebrate the event. This book presents the views that artists immortalized in a range of mediums, attitudes and moods. They range from the prosaic and thoughtful to the surreal and eccentric, and from the truly artistic to the kitsch souvenirs produced for the tourist trade. This volume presents a most interesting and rewarding browsing experience. In 1976 a book of artistic photographs by Henry Mallard, with an introduction by Max Dupain and Howard Tanner, was published, depicting the construction of the Harbour Bridge: *Building the Sydney Harbour Bridge* (Melbourne: Sun Books, 1976).

324 To build a bridge: Glebe Island, Sydney, Australia.
Text by Murray Waldren, Robert Renew, photographs by David Moore. Sydney: Chapter & Verse, 1996. 184p.

This large-format book consists of artistic photographs taken over three years by celebrated photographer David Moore during the construction of the spectacular Glebe Island Bridge. The text discusses the genesis of the bridge and places it in perspective through interviews with supporters, critics and people who designed and built the bridge. There is an additional essay explaining the engineering aspect of this major project, adjudged to be a success because it was completed fifteen months ahead of schedule, with an unblemished safety record.

325 The Stadium, how we built the dream: a photographic essay by Ross Coffey on the construction of Stadium Australia.
Edited by Peter O'Connell, text by Ian Streeter. Sydney: Box Press, 1999. unpaginated.

Stadium Australia is the official name for the Sydney 2000 Olympic Stadium. With a seating capacity of 110,000, it will host the opening and closing ceremonies and track and field athletics. The Stadium was completed in less than two years and more than 6,000 people worked on it during the construction phase. It opened in 1997 and several sporting events have been held there since. Ross Coffey, through his spectacular photography, celebrates the construction of this main venue of the 2000 Olympic Games.

326 Significant sites: history and public works in New South Wales.
Edited by Lenore Coltheart. Sydney: Hale & Iremonger assisted by the Public Works Department of New South Wales, 1989. 192p. maps. bibliog. plans. (Public Works History Series).

This collection of essays is an exploration of the cultural significance of public works. The contributors look at great public works in Sydney from a fresh viewpoint and disciplinary approach. Works examined include: the Parramatta Gaol, the Australian Museum building in the city of Sydney, the Garden Palace built for the Sydney

International Exhibition in 1879, mental health asylums such as Tarban Creek (opened in 1838) and Callan Park at Rozelle (opened in 1883), the NSW Conservatorium of Music, developed from the original Government House Stables next to the Botanic Gardens and finally the only 20th-century edifice to be discussed, the Sydney Harbour Bridge.

327   Australia's first government house.

Helen Proudfoot, Anne Bickford, Brian Egloff, Robyn Stocks. Sydney: Allen & Unwin in conjunction with the Department of Planning, 1991. 196p. maps. bibliog. plans. diagrams.

The book presents the results of the archaeological study, an exercise still rare in Australia, of the building begun by Governor Phillip in May 1788, and the home of Australian Governors for the next half century. It was demolished in the mid-19th century, but in 1983 great public interest was aroused when the foundations were uncovered in what was then a parking lot in the centre of the city. The excavations and study of the site and the historical study that accompanied it makes for absorbing reading. There is a vivid collection of graphic material, excellently reproduced, on every stage of the earliest European building in Australia.

328   Elizabeth Farm, Parramatta: a history and a guide.

James Broadbent.   Sydney: Historic Houses Trust of New South Wales, 1995. rev. ed. 80p. bibliog.

Built in 1793 in Parramatta by John Macarthur (1767-1834), probably the most influential private resident in early New South Wales, and named after his wife, Elizabeth Farm contains part of one of the oldest European buildings in Australia. The house was in continual use as a dwelling for 175 years and was an important social, political and agricultural centre in the first forty years of the colony. Elizabeth Farm is a fine example of early colonial architecture in which can be traced the development of the English-style cottage into the uniquely Australian homestead. It has a garden laid out in the style of the 1830s. Classified by the National Trust, today it is managed by the Historic Houses Trust of New South Wales and is open to the public. The booklet gives a family history of the Macarthurs and describes the architectural evolution of the buildings.

329   Australia's first Parliament: Parliament House, New South Wales.

Edited by Maisy Stapleton.   Sydney: Parliament of New South Wales, 1987. 176p. bibliog.

The Parliament of New South Wales was the first Parliament in Australia. Today it is housed in one of the country's earliest surviving buildings, once part of Sydney's General Hospital. For over 150 years the early hospital building was threatened with demolition, until in the 1970s, a decision was made to retain the oldest sections of Parliament House and to construct a major new building behind it, to cope with overcrowding and modern requirements. This sumptuously produced book, containing many photographs and other illustrative material, has been published to commemorate the restoration of the old parliamentary buildings and the construction of the modern building.

330 A source of inspiration & delight: the building of the State Library of New South Wales since 1826.
David J. Jones.   Sydney: Library Council of New South Wales, 1988. 176p.

A very well illustrated history of the State Library of New South Wales from its 19th-century origins in warehouses, 'dingy caverns' and 'awful dungeons', through to the new, modern complex in Macquarie Street, adjacent to the New South Wales Parliament Building. The emphasis throughout is on the buildings and their architectural aspects, although there is also an account of the development of services and the collections of the Library.

331 Sydney Town hall: a social history.
Margo Beasley.   Sydney: City of Sydney in association with Hale & Iremonger, 1998. 127p. bibliog.

The Sydney Town Hall, headquarters of its municipal government, was built during the boom period in Sydney's development, between 1869 and 1889, to an extravagant scale in the imposing French Second Empire style. It dominated Sydney's commercial heart when it was built, and to this day retains some of that dominance, despite having been surrounded by city skyscrapers. The Town Hall has been at the centre of the city's cultural and political life for over a century and this sumptuously illustrated book captures its history most vividly.

332 The city's centrepiece: the history of the Sydney G.P.O.
Australia Post.   Sydney: Hale & Iremonger, 1988. 114p. bibliog.

The Sydney General Post Office was built at huge expense in stages, from 1866 to 1891, and today it is one of the city's finest public buildings of the 19th century. The 1960s saw an awakening of public interest in the heritage value of historical buildings. Recognizing the public sentiment, Australia Post undertook the immense task of restoring the building and today it stands in Martin Place in its original glory. The book describes the history and architecture of the Post Office. There are many illustrations supporting the text.

333 QVB: an improbable story.
Suzanne Stirling, text by Helen Ivory.   Sydney: Ipoh Ltd, 1998. 96p.

The Queen Victoria Markets Building was originally designed as a grand shopping emporium, based on similar developments in Paris and London, where all the customer's needs could be catered for under one roof. Built on a site adjacent to the Sydney Town Hall, it opened its doors to an excited public in 1898. However, following building alterations in 1918 and 1934 which destroyed the architectural integrity of the interior of the building, from the late 1950s to the early 1980s it continued to fall into disrepair and there were moves to demolish it and use the site for other purposes. Finally, in a cooperative venture between the City Council and a commercial developer, it was decided to restore the building to its original state and purpose. It was reopened in 1986 as a shopping mall and this book celebrates in text and with historical as well as contemporary photographs the centennial of one of Sydney's great buildings.

334 The Strand Arcade: a history.
Barbara Salisbury. Sydney: Hale & Iremonger, 1990. 111p.

The Strand Arcade was opened as a shopping venture in 1892. It was the fifth and last arcade built in Victorian Sydney. After several fires and threats of demolition in the 1970s, it was completely restored to its original condition and opened its doors as a speciality shopping arcade in November 1978. Today it is the only arcade remaining in its original form in Sydney. The book is richly illustrated.

335 The lions of Retreat Street: a Chinese temple in inner Sydney.
Edited by Ann Stephen. Sydney: Powerhouse Publishing and Hale & Iremonger, 1997. 80p. maps. bibliog.

The Yin Ming Temple was built in 1908 in the inner industrial suburb of Alexandria to serve the Chinese community who worked in the market gardens around Botany Bay. The temple is an excellent example of traditional Chinese architecture in transition, displaying various adaptations to local conditions and materials. It is one of only nine surviving Chinese temples in Australia. The book examines the architecture of the building, its objects and the present-day members of the Yin Ming Temple society who have maintained the temple, its traditions and rituals. Photographs and plans accompany the text.

336 Building for nature: Walter Burley Griffin and Castlecrag.
Meredith Walker, Adrienne Kabos, James Weirick. Sydney: Walter Burley Griffin Society, 1994. 80p. maps. bibliog. plans.

American architect Walter Burley Griffin, married to another architect, Marion Lucy Mahony, won the international competition for the design of the Australian capital Canberra in 1912. He moved to Australia to take charge of the project, but resigned in 1920. In 1924 he transferred to Sydney to develop Castlecrag, a residential community designed to preserve the natural environment of a bushland promontory on the foreshores of Middle Harbour. His houses of rock and patterned concrete blocks of his own design were widely regarded as eccentric and at the time of his death in 1937, only 19 of the planned 300 houses had been completed. This book provides the history of the Castlecrag development, describes in text and pictures fourteen of the houses completed and makes suggestions for the conservation of the Griffith legacy.

337 Francis Greenway: architect.
James Broadbent, Joy Hughes. Sydney: Historic Houses Trust of New South Wales, 1997. 112p. bibliog.

Francis Greenway (1777-1837) was Australia's first Government Architect. A convicted forger, he was transported and arrived in Sydney in 1814, and in 1816 Governor Macquarie appointed him Acting Civil Architect. For seven years he realized the Governor's schemes for public works that raised Sydney from a convict outpost to a thriving township. After quarrelling with the Governor, Greenway continued in private practice, designing houses and stores for prosperous Sydney merchants. In this handsomely produced book, the authors present Greenway's work in text and excellent supporting illustrations and drawings of plans. Although many of the buildings have been demolished, a map of the town of Sydney in 1831 indicates the sites where the buildings stood. In 1980 *Francis Greenway: a celebration* introduced by J. M. Freeland was published (North Ryde, New South Wales: Cassell Australia, 1980. 135p.), featuring photographs of Greenway's work by the celebrated photographer Max Dupain.

338 The golden decade of Australian architecture: the work of John Verge.
Text by James Broadbent, Ian Evans, Clive Lucas, photographs by Max Dupain. Sydney: David Ell Press in association with the Elizabeth Bay House Trust, 1978. 128p.

The architect John Verge (1782-1861) arrived in Sydney from England in 1828, intending to become a pastoralist. However, economic necessity forced Verge back to his old profession. From 1830 for seven years he and an associate, John Bibb, who joined him in 1832, turned out more than 100 fine buildings, some, including Elizabeth Bay House on the shores of Sydney Harbour, still standing today as witnesses to his architectural genius. The book is a tribute to Verge, surveying his work in text and ninety superb photographs by Max Dupain, Australia's leading architectural photographer. Also included are eleven of Verge's building plans.

339 The sleeping city: the story of Rookwood Necropolis.
Edited by David A. Weston, photographs and maps by Joan Sigrist, project co-ordinator Laurel Burge. Sydney: Society of Australian Genealogists in conjunction with Friends of Rookwood, 1997. 160p. bibliog.

A reprint of a work first published in 1989, this resulted from the project of the Society of the Australian Genealogists to record the grave sites of Rookwood Cemetery. This large-format book examines various forms of the 'sleeping city'. The text considers architectural styles, stonemasons and landscape and design, as well as gravestone inscriptions. There are maps of the site, illustrations and photographs, a number in colour, appendices listing wildlife recorded at Rookwood, a bibliography and an index. The cemetery was established in 1867. Today, it is the largest Victorian cemetery in the world and continues to reflect 19th-century attitudes to death and mourning.

340 Avalon landscape & harmony: Walter Burley Griffin, Alexander Stewart Jolly & Harry Ruskin Rowe.
Edited by Jan Roberts. Sydney: Ruskin Rowe Press, 1999. 104p. bibliog. plans.

This book celebrates the organic architectural tradition and artistic life of Avalon, centre of Sydney's northern peninsula. The author begins with an introduction to the neighbourhood, which was first subdivided during the 1920s, and concludes with a documentation of the thoughts of organic architect Richard Leplastrier, who has lived in the area for forty-five years. Other essays explain the local activities of three architects: Walter Burley Griffin (by Ian Stephenson), Alexander Stewart Jolley (by Maisy Stapleton) and Harry Ruskin Rowe (by Janine Formica and Caroline Kades). The book is richly illustrated with photographs, sketches and plans.

341   Sydney lace: ornamental cast iron in architecture in Sydney.
E. Graeme Robertson.   Melbourne: Georgian House, 1962. 198p.

This volume continues the author's work in other books on the use of cast iron ornamentation in Australian architecture. Robertson argues that the use of cast iron in Sydney and Melbourne and other Australian cities competes in interest with that anywhere in the world and he laments the destruction of this form of architectural embellishment. The Sydney volume is essentially a record of what can still be seen in Sydney. The beautiful photographs tell their own story and the text is devoted mainly to historical detail.

342   Centennial Park: a history.
Paul Ashton, Kate Blackmore, contemporary photography by John Gollings.   Sydney: NSWU Press, 1988. 152p. bibliog.

A suburb and a large park in Eastern Sydney, Centennial Park was reclaimed from swampland (once the source of Sydney's water supply) and established in 1888 to celebrate 100 years of British settlement in Australia. This book, not a full history of the Park despite the subtitle, celebrates the centenary of the Park. Although development has encroached on parts of it over the last 100 years, the Park today has become one of the most beautiful havens in an overcrowded city, used by large numbers of Sydney's citizens for various recreational purposes. The book is enhanced by many historical photographs. In comparison, the modern photography appears very stark and sombre and out of character with the book.

343   Discovering the Domain.
Edited by Edwin Wilson, research by Shirley Colless.   Sydney: Hale & Iremonger, 1986. 64p. maps.

The Domain began as the Governor's private preserve soon after the arrival of the First Fleet in 1788. With the establishment of responsible government in 1856, its control passed from the Governor to a public body and it soon became a priceless large open space, superbly located on the Harbour and adjacent to the City of Sydney. Before long, sporting activities, political meetings and ceremonial occasions began to take place in the Domain. The tradition continues today with various cultural events such as opera, ballet and symphony concerts being performed in the open. This book is an illustrated account of the development of the Domain – 'Sydney's lungs' – over 200 years. For an account of soapbox oratory at the Domain, always a popular Sunday event, the reader may consult Stephen Maxwell's *The history of soapbox oratory. Part one. Prominent speakers of the Sydney Domain* (Chiswick, New South Wales: Published by the Author, 1994).

344   Gardens in bloom: Jocelyn Brown and her Sydney gardens of the '30s and '40s.
Helen Proudfoot.   Sydney: Kangaroo Press, 1989. 124p. bibliog. plans.

The 1930s and 1940s were the great decades of the flower garden in Australia. Jocelyn Brown was an influential garden writer and designer during this period. Her gardens form part of the design history of these years. The garden, as she saw it, was made to form a creative ensemble with the domestic architecture, but it was to be more than just a frame for the house, it was to be a place to spend time in. It would play the role of an 'outdoor room' in which the balmy climate of Sydney could be enjoyed. In this book Brown's gardens and planning programmes are described in detail and the text is accompanied by many photographs and her plans for garden designs.

The Arts

345   The innovators: the Sydney alternatives in the rise of modern art, literature and ideas.
Geoffrey Dutton.   Melbourne: Macmillan, 1986. 266p. bibliog.

A chatty, anecdotal exposé of the Sydney arts and literary scene from the 1930s to the late 1960s by Australia's much published 'man of letters', Geoffrey Dutton. His thesis is that Sydney is a city where an effervescent spirit of artistic and literary innovation is fostered by the kind of place Sydney is.

346   Making Australian art 1916-49: Sydney Ure Smith, patron and publisher.
Nancy D. H. Underhill.   Melbourne: Oxford University Press, 1991. 311p. bibliog.

Sydney Ure Smith (1887-1949), printmaker, graphic designer, founding publisher and editor of the influential 1920s and 1930s magazines *Art in Australia* and *Home* and book publisher, became the foremost supporter of Australian art, patronising through his various business ventures many of the foremost artists of the day. This book is not a formal biography of Ure Smith, but discusses mainly his influence on the Sydney art world of his day. The text can sometimes be difficult, because of the book's origin as a doctoral thesis, but it makes a valuable contribution to Australian art studies.

347   The Sydney art patronage system 1890-1940.
Heather Johnson.   Sydney: Bungoona Technologies, 1997. 279p. bibliog.

A detailed examination of art patronage, an important aspect of art production. The author, an art historian, shows that in the period covered by the book the art patronage network pivoted around the Art Gallery of New South Wales, which remained the most important promoter and endorser of art in Sydney. After the First World War and the ensuing economic boom, there was a flowering of art societies, independent dealers, private galleries and private patrons, which are all discussed in turn. The author concludes that they all remained closely dependent on the State Gallery to validate their activities. There are a number of black-and-white illustrations.

348 AGNSW collections.

Sydney: The Art Gallery of New South Wales, 1994. 287p.

The Art Gallery of New South Wales is the second oldest state gallery in Australia, established in 1874 with the aid of a government grant. It is situated in parkland adjacent to Sydney's Central Business District and is by far the most visited museum in the country, attracting around a million visitors each year. The present volume, published in large format, surveys the most significant holdings in all curatorial departments. It contains 325 colour plates and besides the director's introduction, is divided in four sections: Australian art, European art, Asian art and contemporary art, compiled by a team of ten curatorial staff members. Overall, it is a summary and historical survey, rather than a complete catalogue of the collection.

349 Decorative arts and design from the Powerhouse Museum.

Powerhouse Museum.   Sydney: Powerhouse Publishing, 1991. 194p. bibliog.

This large-format, richly illustrated volume presents the Museum's decorative art and design objects collected over the past 110 years. The book is researched and written by the curatorial staff and, as well as the 200 illustrations of objects in the collection, it provides an account of the historical and cultural context in which the collection has developed. The Museum of Applied Arts and Science, popularly known as the Powerhouse, is Sydney's and Australia's largest museum and should be any tourist's highlight on their visit to Sydney.

350 Absolutely Mardi Gras: costume and design of the Sydney Gay & Lesbian Mardi Gras.

Robert Swieca.   Sydney: Powerhouse Publishing and Doubleday, 1997. 106p.

The annual Sydney Gay and Lesbian Mardi Gras parade and festival have become world famous. The parade is a noisy and colourful spectacle notable for its flamboyant floats and outrageous costumes. This book focuses on the extraordinary costumes made for Mardi Gras in text and colour photographs, covering twenty years of the parade.

351 Early Sydney moderns: John Young and the Macquarie Galleries 1916-1946.

Jean Campbell.   Sydney: Craftsman House, 1988. 203p.

John Young was an influential figure on the Sydney art scene for thirty years until his death in 1946. In 1925 he was co-founder of the Macquarie Galleries. The inaugural exhibition concerned the avant-garde paintings of Roland Wakelin and in conformity with this precedent, later exhibitions featured much of the Sydney modernists' art of the 1920s. The only commercial art gallery in Sydney to survive the depression years, the gallery became an institution exercising great influence on art in Sydney and its exhibitions launched many artists on successful careers. The author, the daughter of John Young, is an art critic and author of other books on Australian art. The book is mainly based on the records of the Macquarie Galleries and interviews with artists and other people active in the Sydney art scene.

352   Bohemians in the bush: the artists' camps of Mosman.
Text by Albie Thoms, edited by Barry Pearce, Linda Slutzkin.
Sydney: Art Gallery of New South Wales, 1991. 80p. bibliog.

This book is based on an exhibition of paintings held at the Art Gallery of New South Wales to celebrate the centenary of the founding of Curlew camp at Little Sirius Cove in Mosman on Sydney Harbour. Many of the masterpieces of Australian Impressionism were painted here by such masters as Julian Ashton, Charles Conder, Tom Roberts and Arthur Streeton. Besides a scholarly text, the book contains twenty-eight reproductions of paintings in colour and historic photographs of the artists at work and everyday life in the camp.

353   The first gallery in Paddington: the artists and their work tell the story of Rudy Komon Art Gallery.
Sydney: Edwards & Shaw, 1981. 72p.

A tribute to Rudy Komon and his Art Gallery, established by Komon in 1959 in a former wine shop in the Sydney inner suburb of Paddington. Komon introduced European methods of full-scale patronage for his artists, unknown in Australia at the time. Until his death in 1982, Komon and the Gallery played an important role in promoting art and artists in Sydney.

354   The Windsor Group 1935-1945: an account of nine young Sydney artists who painted in Woolloomooloo, the inner city and the Hawkesbury area – Emu Plains, Richmond and especially Windsor.
Introduction by Bernard Smith, with an account of the Group by Roderick Shaw.   Sydney: Edwards & Shaw, 1989. 48p.

Members of the Windsor Group chose as their subjects inner Sydney buildings or 'slums', usually not considered suitable subjects for art. As Professor Bernard Smith says in the preface: 'The Windsor Group may ... be seen as part of a significant trend in Australian painting that began to emerge in the years immediately prior to the Second World War, when artists began to turn away from the dominance of pastoral landscape in a new awareness of the urban environment'.

355   The art of the First Fleet and other early Australian drawings.
Edited by Bernard Smith, Alwyne Wheeler.   Melbourne: Oxford University Press in association with the Australian Academy of the Humanities and the British Museum (Natural History), 1988. 256p. maps. bibliog.

This scholarly study contains many little-known works of art from the voyage of the First Fleet and from the early years of settlement at Sydney Cove, selected from more than 600 drawings and paintings held in the British Museum. Included are the first original depictions of Australian Aborigines in the Sydney region by European artists, the earliest drawings of certain plants, birds, mammals and fishes, and early renderings of the settlement at Sydney Cove. Five chapters of text, written by authorities in their field, supplement the lavish illustrations in this large-format volume.

356 Joseph Lycett: Governor Macquarie's convict artist.
John Turner.   Newcastle, New South Wales: Hunter History
Publications, 1997. 148p. bibliog.

Convicted for forgery in 1811, Lycett arrived in Sydney in 1814. During his sojourn in New South Wales he made numerous paintings and drawings including landscapes (many with Aborigines), views of Sydney and the mansions built by the free settlers, as well as a few botanical drawings. After his return to England in 1823, he prepared and published the fifty aquatints in his *Views in Australia and Van Diemen's Land, 1824-25* (London: J. Souter, 1825; Melbourne: Thomas Nelson, 1971).

Performing Arts

357 Theatre comes to Australia.
Eric Irvin.   Brisbane: University of Queensland Press, 1971. 260p.
bibliog.

This is the detailed story of Australia's first permanent theatre – Sydney's Theatre Royal, established by the first free Jewish settler in the colony, Barnett Levey. The Theatre Royal was in effect an English provincial theatre of the late 1820s transplanted to Sydney. It put on the same 18th- and 19th-century plays and the stage and acting techniques were the same as in the English provinces, Scotland, Wales, Ireland and America. The story of the Theatre Royal is told against the background of colonial Sydney of 1828-38. Levey died in 1837 and in 1840 the building, no longer used as a theatre, burned down. An appendix lists every play presented at the theatre during the period 1823-38.

358 The romance of the Sydney stage.
OSRIC, Humphrey Holl, Alfred John Cripps.   Sydney: Currency
Press in association with National Library of Australia, 1996. 323p.
bibliog.

The manuscript of this book was written in the first decade of the 20th century by two Sydney journalists, one of whom, Humphrey Hall, was also an unsuccessful playwright. The book provides an account of theatre in Sydney from 1788 to 1861, but most of the text is devoted to the last twenty years of this period. The diversity of theatrical offerings, such as Italian operas, Shakespeare and other serious drama, concerts and oratorios, is impressive and gives lie to the myth that 19th-century Australia was a cultural desert. The manuscript was written in a lively, journalistic style and is well structured and only minor changes have been made to the published text. An annotated list of more than 700 plays and operas performed during the period appears at the end of the book. There are also reproductions of contemporary illustrations.

359 The story of the Theatre Royal.
Ian Bevan. Sydney: Currency Press, 1993. 266p. bibliog.

More than any other theatre, Sydney's Theatre Royal embodies the history of popular entertainment in Australia. The first Theatre Royal opened in 1832 and the author traces its story through 160 years of triumphs and disasters and four separate buildings to the present, when it survives on slick, imported musicals, like *Cats, Les Misérables* and *The Phantom of the Opera.* Written in a brisk entertaining style, the book also contains a chronological list of all performances from 1875 to 1993.

360 Not without dust & heat – my life in the theatre.
Doris Fitton. Sydney: Harper & Row, 1981. 200p.

In this autobiography, Doris Fitton tells two life stories – her own and that of the Independent Theatre which she founded in 1930. Until its demise in 1977, it catered for the theatre lovers of Sydney with the best of Australian and overseas drama and through its School of Dramatic Art trained many young actors, producers, stage technicians and playwrights. The book describes in a chatty, anecdotal way not only the plays produced and personalities associated with the Independent, but also the Sydney theatre scene in general. The book includes a list of major productions at the Independent from 1930 until 1977. Sadly, there is no index, which in a book of this nature is quite indispensable.

361 Ten on the Tote.
Compiled by Josephine South, text by Harry Scott. Sydney: Old Tote Theatre Company, 1973. 64p.

A large-format, illustrated history of the Old Tote Theatre Company to celebrate its tenth anniversary. After moving to the new Drama Theatre at the Sydney Opera House in the 1980s, the Old Tote collapsed and re-emerged as the Sydney Theatre Company.

362 The New years 1932-: the plays, people and events of six decades of Sydney's radical New Theatre.
Sydney: The Theatre, 1992. rev. ed. 36p.

Formed in 1932, Sydney New Theatre is now Australia's oldest continuously performing theatre, professional or amateur. Its roots are to be found in workers' arts movements and left-wing politics. Today the New Theatre's policy is: 'To continue its role as a socially relevant and committed theatre'. This booklet presents a history of its first, often turbulent, sixty years of operation, together with a list of productions since 1933.

363 Sydney Opera House: from the outside in.
Jill Sykes. Sydney: Playbill and Sydney Opera House Trust, 1993. 192p.

This is a large-format, lavishly produced book about Sydney's internationally renowned Opera House. Although the narrative includes the controversies surrounding the building's construction, the emphasis is on the activities in the performance spaces: the Concert Hall, seating 2,679 people; the Opera Theatre, seating 1,547; the Drama Theatre, seating 544; and the Playhouse, seating 398. The text is complemented with coloured photographs of performances and performers which have been given in the different venues, including orchestral concerts, operas, dance, plays, chamber music, jazz, musicals, pop concerts and a host of other entertainment. Also shown are the restaurants, tourist vantage points and artworks. Altogether, the book provides a complete view of the Opera House as a working centre for the performing arts and one of Australia's most popular tourist attractions.

364 The strange case of Eugene Goossens and other tales from the Opera House.
Ava Hubble. Sydney: Collins, 1988. 280p.

The author was Press Officer of the Sydney Opera House for fifteen years since 1972. In this book she raises the curtain on life backstage in the Opera House. The narrative is full of interesting anecdotes of the people connected with the building: the architects, the bureaucrats, the politicians, the workers and, of course, the performers. Also included are exclusive interviews with Joern Utzon, the designer-architect, in which he reveals his feelings about the treatment he received from Australian politicians and bureaucrats at the time of the construction of the building, which makes for very interesting reading indeed. In 1983 Hubble published a more formal, copiously illustrated book about the first fifteen years of the Opera House, entitled *More than an Opera House* (Sydney: Lansdowne Press, 1983. 176p.).

365 Play on! 60 years of music making with the Sydney Symphony Orchestra.
Phillip Sametz. Sydney: ABC Enterprises, 1992. 376p. bibliog.

This readable, comprehensive history of the Sydney Symphony Orchestra was written by the editorial manager for ABC concerts and published to coincide with the Australian Broadcasting Corporation's sixtieth anniversary. The text is enhanced with many black-and-white photographs.

366 Music for a hundred years: the story of the House of Paling.
Eve Keane. Sydney: Oswald Ziegler Publications, 1954. 76p.

William Paling arrived in Sydney in 1853 from Holland. Having had a musical education, he soon became prominent in the musical life of Sydney, arranging and participating in concerts and teaching music. He also opened a music shop, which became a Sydney institution. Many visiting and local musical performers treated it as a kind of a club. This book provides the main facts of the music business of Palings, but also comprises a story of musical life in Sydney with an appendix listing world celebrities who toured Australia between 1933 and 1953, many of them closely associated with Palings.

367 Meet me at the Trocadero.
Joan Ford. Cowra, New South Wales: Published by the Author, 1995. 218p. bibliog.

The Sydney Trocadero opened in 1936 and closed in 1971. It was a restaurant/dance hall, with a capacity for 2,000 people, and an entertainment centre for Sydneysiders for thirty-five years. This book relates the story of the Trocadero and the musicians and bands associated with it. The author is the daughter of Frank Coughlan, trombonist and bandleader, composer and jazz pioneer, whose name was synonymous with the Trocadero. His discography is included in the book, which is also a tribute to Coughlan's and his family's place in the musical history of Australia. The book is available from Joan Ford, P.O. Box 774, Cowra, New South Wales 2794.

368   Sex and thugs and rock'n'roll': a year in Kings Cross 1963-1964.
Billy Thorpe.   Sydney: Pan Macmillan, 1996. 390p.

This is the story of one year in the life of Billy Thorpe of the rock group, the Aztecs. It tells of the formation of the Aztecs and their rise to the top of the pop charts by the end of 1964 with the hit 'Poison Ivy'. It also portrays vividly the social and low life in Kings Cross, Sydney's equivalent to Soho, a place of strip joints, prostitution, hectic night life and criminal activity. Written in a racy style, it reads better than many a crime novel.

369   Ubu Films: Sydney underground movies 1965-1970.
Peter Mudie.   Sydney: UNSW Press, 1997. 287p. bibliog.

The book is a chronicle of the activities of the Ubu film group of Sydney through the 1965-70 period. Ubu Films was Australia's first group devoted to making experimental films and the first organization to establish an extensive network for the exhibition and distribution of independent films. Ubu produced Australia's first light shows and published its first underground newspaper *Ubunews*. The primary material, such as excerpts from the underground press, is interestingly juxtaposed with commentary and reviews of the same events in the mainstream press. There is a wealth of visual material: film frames, photographs, cartoons, underground posters, programmes and manifestos. It is a very interesting compilation for the film buff as well as the film student and has much to offer to the general reader.

Sport and Recreation

370   Bid: how Australia won the 2000 Games.
Rod McGeoch with Glenda Korporaal.   Sydney: Heinemann, 1994. 335p.

This is the story of how Sydney won the right to hold the 2000 Olympic Games, by the bid team's Chief Executive Officer Rod McGeoch, with assistance from senior finance journalist Glenda Korporaal. The emphasis throughout the book is on the role played by marketing and the sales techniques used to secure the bid.

371   Staging the Olympics: the event and its impact.
Edited by Richard Cashman, Anthony Hughes.   Sydney: UNSW Press, 1999. 226p. bibliog.

This book is the first to provide an overview of how Sydney is progressing in staging the 2000 Olympic Games. Contributors include academics and people involved in the Games planning process concerning marketing, media, security, tourism, transport and volunteers. Topics covered include the bid process, the costs and benefits of staging the Olympics, the impact on environment, urban design, drugs, cultural Olympiad, handling the media and the Paralympics. The Centre for Olympic Studies at the University of New South Wales has published a series of reports, such as *Forum on the impacts of the Olympics,* in 1997 and *The green Games: a golden opportunity,* 1997, amongst others.

372   Their chastity was not too rigid: leisure times in early Australia.
J. W. C. Cumes.   Melbourne: Longman Cheshire Reed, 1979. 378p. bibliog.

The first book to be entirely devoted to the leisure activities of the convicts and early settlers from 1788 to the gold rush days in the 1850s. The emphasis is on New South Wales and Sydney.

373   The principal club: a history of the Australian Jockey Club.
Martin Painter, Richard Waterhouse.   Sydney: Allen & Unwin,
1992. 252p. bibliog.

Horseracing is very popular and is a multi-million dollar industry in Australia. The
Australian Jockey Club (AJC) is the ruling body for the sport in the state of New South
Wales and distributes large amounts of money and is responsible for the livelihoods of
thousands of individuals. For these reasons the AJC has always been part of the Sydney
political as well as social landscape. The present book is the first academic history of an
Australian horse racing club. A wealth of illustrations accompany the text.

**374   Gentlemen of the Australian turf: their bets, their bankrolls and
their bankruptcies.**
David Hickie.   Sydney: Angus & Robertson, 1986. 418p.

Horseracing and betting are popular Australian pastimes. Going to the races is an
enduring social tradition. In this book journalist and author David Hickie presents a
cavalcade of 'colourful racing identities', including legendary punters, leviathan bookies,
shady characters, race callers, famous horse owners, as well as jockeys and trainers,
which give Australian horseracing so much of its excitement. Throughout the book the
emphasis is on the Sydney scene over the past 150 years.

375   Early cricket in Sydney 1803 to 1856.
Jas Scott, edited by Richard Cashman, Stephen Gibbs.   Sydney:
New South Wales Cricket Association, 1991. 243p. bibliog.

The book deals with the most neglected area of the history of Australian cricket, the
beginnings and growth of the game of cricket to the time when inter-colonial competition
began. The book is meticulously researched and contains many lengthy quotations from
contemporary newspapers. There are a number of original illustrations.

**376   80 not out: a celebration of test cricket at the Sydney Cricket
ground.**
Philip Derriman.   Sydney: Playbill, 1994. 121p.

The first Test was played at the Sydney Cricket Ground in February 1882 between
Australia and England. Up to and including the Test series against the West Indies in
1992-93, Australia played eighty Tests on the Sydney Ground; it won forty of them, lost
twenty-five and drew fifteen. The book describes the action over more than 100 years and
also gives a detailed statistical analysis of the games played. Derriman also wrote *The
grand old ground, a history of the Sydney Cricket Ground* (North Ryde, New South
Wales: Cassell Australia, 1981. 150p.) and *True to the blue, a history of the New South
Wales Cricket Association* ([Mosman, New South Wales]: Richard Smart Publishing,
1985. 245p.).

377   They ran with the ball: how Rugby football began in Australia.
Thomas V. Hickie.   Melbourne: Longman Cheshire, 1993. 243p.
bibliog.

The author documents the first reports of football games in Sydney in 1829 and takes the
story up to 1874 when the Southern Rugby Football Union was formed in Sydney. Sydney

and New South Wales are still the centre for the game today although it is played in all states of Australia.

378 True blue: the story of the NSW Rugby League.
Ian Heads. Sydney: Ironbark Press, 1992. 495p.

Rugby League is the most popular football sport in Sydney. This large-format, illustrated book marks Rugby League's eighty-fifth season in Sydney, since its split from Rugby Union in 1907. It tells the story of the game in terms of the great players and great games, not neglecting the administrative role of the NSW Rugby League.

379 March of the dragons: the story of St. George Rugby League Club.
Ian Heads, edited by Larry Writer. Sydney: Lester-Townsend, 1989. 204p.

The St George Rugby League Club won eleven successive premierships during the period 1956-66, a world record. This large-format, illustrated volume traces the history of the club since its formation in 1921. The story of the Dragons' eleven-year golden era is told in Larry Writer's *Never before, never again* (Sydney: Pan Macmillan, 1995. 457p.), which also contains the reflections on football and life of sixteen key St George men and the families of two, who have died. Together, the books provide an insight into one of Sydney's most successful Rugby League clubs.

380 The mighty Bears! A social history of North Sydney Rugby League.
Andrew Moore, statistics by David Middleton. Sydney: Macmillan for North Sydney Rugby League Club, 1996. 592p. bibliog.

This book is not just the story of a football club, but is also a detailed social and political analysis of the district of North Sydney and its close relation to its major rugby league football club. The author, a historian and league enthusiast, compares North Sydney's sometimes radical working-class past with its trendy present and increasingly bourgeois future. The book is easy to read, replete with anecdotes and is well illustrated.

381 A sense of union: a history of the Sydney University Football Club.
Thomas V. Hickie. Sydney: Playright Publishing, 1998. 380p. bibliog. tables.

The Sydney University Football Club is Australia's oldest rugby union football club as well as being the eighth oldest rugby club in the world and the oldest outside Britain and Ireland. It has produced ninety-three Australian representatives and won thirty-three first grade premierships since the formation of the New South Wales Rugby Union in 1870. The author, a lawyer and sport historian, was General Manager of the Sydney University Football Club from 1995 to 1998. He has written a history of the club which does not merely recite statistics of players and games, but focuses on issues and tries to capture the spirit of a successful club.

382 Flying north for the winter: the story of the Sydney Swans.
Sally Freud, Mark Cuttler. Sydney: Random House, 1999. 184p. bibliog. tables.

Australian Rules football is a fast, spectacular game played between teams of eighteen players. Invented locally, it is the dominant football sport in most Australian States except New South Wales, where for many decades the game of Rugby League reigned supreme. In order to promote the game of Australian Rules football nationwide, the South Melbourne Football Club, formed in Melbourne nearly 130 years ago, moved to Sydney in 1982 to become known as the Sydney Swans. This book tells the story of the Club with the emphasis on the Sydney years. Another book about the club is Jim Main's *Plugger and the mighty Swans* (Melbourne: Information Australia, 1996. 292p.).

383 The story of golf in New South Wales 1851-1987.
David J. Innes. Sydney: New South Wales Golf Association, 1988. 312p.

With its wide open spaces and balmy climate, enabling golf courses to be built in great numbers around the country, Australia has become one of golf's power bases. This book documents the rich golfing tradition of New South Wales and Sydney, where well-known international events are conducted annually. Two of the more venerated golf clubs have published their own histories. They are: *Ten decades: 1882-1982: a story of the events which go to make the history of 100 years of the Australian Golf Club,* by John Alenson ([Sydney]: Australian Golf Club, 1982. 215p.); and *The Royal Sydney Golf Club: the first hundred years,* by Colin Tatz and Brian Stoddart (St Leonards, New South Wales: Allen & Unwin, 1993. 284p.).

384 Boxing Day: the fight that changed the world.
Jeff Wells. Sydney: HarperCollins, 1998. 245p.

This is the gripping tale of the first boxing match in the world that pitted white against black in a heavyweight championship bout. The antagonists were Jack Johnson, a black American and white Canadian Tommy Burns, and the fight took place on 26 December 1908, in front of 20,000 spectators in a timber stadium by Sydney Harbour. The book is more than a sporting story; it provides details of the social background of the times, showing the bigotry and xenophobia that permeated Australian and Sydney society in the first decade of the 20th century. The book is well-written by an experienced journalist, but lacks an index and a bibliography.

385 The battlers: the history of Ashfield Bowling Club.
Geoff Howe. Sydney: Ancestral Trail Publications, 1998. 96p. bibliog.

The New South Wales Bowling Association, the world's oldest bowling association, was formed on 22 May 1880 with four foundation clubs. Today, the game of lawn bowls is played widely in each state of Australia and Sydney has hundreds of clubs in all suburbs. This booklet presents the history of one such club in the Sydney suburb of Ashfield. The author, a trained historian, has written a compact history of the club, reflecting similar experiences in other Sydney clubs, which are centres for the recreational activities of thousands of Sydneysiders, particularly the elderly.

386 The 50th Sydney–Hobart ocean racing classic: Melbourne–Hobart 1994.
Richard Bennett, text by Bob Ross.   Hobart, Tasmania: Richard Bennett, 1995. 96p. map.

The Sydney–Hobart yacht race started in 1945 and has become an annual event and the principal ocean race in Australia. The start of the race on Boxing Day attracts thousands of spectators along the Sydney Harbour foreshores and hundreds of boats on the water. This book commemorates the fiftieth anniversary race in 1994. It briefly tells the story of the yachts at sea. A similar book, without the dramatic colour photographs of Bennett, is *Sydney to Hobart: the 1994 golden commemorative Sydney to Hobart Yacht race log* (Maroochydore, Queensland: MDL Publishing, 1994. 127p.). This book provides a brief history of each of the fifty races. Rob Mundle's *Fatal storm: the 54th Sydney to Hobart yacht race* (Pymble, New South Wales: HarperCollins, 1999. 319p.) provides an account of the 1998 race, which became a major sporting disaster. Six sailors perished and numerous yachts sank or were badly damaged.

387 A century of Sydney's flying sailors.
Margaret Molloy.   Sydney: Sydney Flying Squadron, 1991. 108p

With its harbour and extensive waterways, Sydney is a sailor's paradise and on weekends there may be thousands of boats of various shapes and sizes on the water. This book is a richly-illustrated presentation of 100 years of the Sydney Flying Squadron, a sailing club. Other club histories are: *Sydney sails: the story of the Royal Sydney Yacht Squadron's first 100 years (1862-1962)*, by P. R. Stephensen (Sydney: Angus & Robertson, 1962. 272p.); and *The amateurs: the second century begins 1972-1997*, edited by John Ferguson (Sydney: Maritime Heritage Press, 1997. 144p.). All books are richly illustrated, depicting the boats under racing conditions, Sydney Harbour and its foreshores.

388 The blue-water bushmen: the colourful story of Australia's best and boldest boatmen.
Bruce Stannard.   Sydney: Angus & Robertson, 1981. 41p. photographs.

By the mid-19th century Sydney is said to have had more amateur and professional sailors than any other city in the world. Sydney Harbour swarmed with every size of open boat and racing became very popular. This book presents the story of those colourful days. A highlight of the book is some 130 full-page black-and-white historic photographs of racing action on Sydney Harbour.

389 The boatshed on Blackwattle Bay: Glebe Rowing Club 1879-1993.
Max Solling.   Sydney: Glebe Rowing Club, 1993. 244p. bibliog.

With Sydney Harbour and its many waterways permeating the metropolis, watersports are very popular in Sydney. This book celebrates the history of the second oldest rowing club in Sydney, that of the old inner city working-class, now gentrified, suburb of Glebe. The book is not the usual recitation of individuals and races, but delves into the social background of Glebe and its residents. A history of the oldest rowing club is to be found in A. L. May's *Sydney rows: a centennial history of the Sydney Rowing Club* ([Abbotsford, New South Wales]: Sydney Rowing Club, 1970. 206p.).

Food and Drink

390 From scarcity to surfeit: a history of food and nutrition in New South Wales.
Robin Walker, Dave Roberts. Sydney: NSWU Press, 1988. 202p. bibliog. tables. graphs.

This book tells the story of the transition from a starving convict population at Sydney Cove in the late 18th century to the one today, where over-indulgence and incorrect eating habits have replaced under-nutrition as a cause of ill health in the community. The book should appeal to general readers as well as to students and researchers.

391 The SBS eating guide to Sydney 1998: a guide to Sydney's world of restaurants, cafes and food shops.
Maeve O'Meara, Joanna Saville. Sydney: Allen & Unwin, 1998. 5th ed. 328p.

The Special Broadcasting Service's latest, extensively expanded edition lists the best ethnic restaurants, cafés, delicatessens and bakeries in Sydney and its suburbs. Eateries and shops are listed by national cuisine in more than forty sections, ranging from African and Italian to Thai and Japanese. Visitors from anywhere in the world should be able to discover their home cooking in these pages.

392 The Sydney Morning Herald 2000 good food guide.
Terry Durack, Jill Dupleix. Melbourne: Anne O'Donovan, 1999. 15th ed. 230p. maps.

Modern Australian cuisine is unique in the world – it combines elements of European cooking with Asian flavours and should be experienced by all visitors to Australia. The 1999 edition of the Sydney Morning Herald's restaurant guide lists over 400 of the best restaurants, hotel dining rooms, bistros, bars and cafés around Sydney. It contains maps with locations of all eating places listed in the guide and there is an index by type of cuisine. There are also gradings of the best restaurants, good value places and eateries with good wine lists. This is an indispensable guide for the 'foodie' and others interested in eating well in Sydney.

393   Cheap eats: Sydney's best restaurant guide. 1999 ed.
Edited by Melita Similovic.   Sydney: Universal Consumer Guides,
1999. 18th ed. 181p.

Now in its eighteenth edition, this is a popular guide to good, inexpensive restaurants in
Sydney and its suburbs. There are useful indexes listing eateries by cuisine, suburb,
outdoor dining, restaurants serving breakfasts and those providing entertainment. The
guide is recommended for the resident as well as the visitor and tourist.

394   Rockpool.
Neil Perry, photographs by Petrina Tinslay.   Melbourne:
Heinemann, 1996. 263p.

Since its beginnings in the late 1980s, Neil Perry's award-winning restaurant, Rockpool,
has remained among the top restaurants in Sydney. Perry has redefined Australian cuisine
by using the quality and range of local produce and combining European tradition with
Asian techniques in the preparation of memorable meals. In this book Perry shares more
than 100 of his recipes with the reader, all suitable for the domestic kitchen. He also
explains his own culinary philosophy.

395   Australia and New Zealand wine companion: 1999 edition.
James Halliday.   Sydney: HarperCollins, 1998. 510p. map.

Although this wine directory is not Sydney related, it is the ideal companion and guide to
people dining out in Sydney or buying a bottle of the local product. In addition to rating
wineries according to quality and value, major winery entries, arranged alphabetically,
include reviews of recommended wines. Similar guides providing ratings for Australian
wines are: *The Penguin good Australian wine guide*, by Mark Shield and Huon Hooke
(Ringwood, Victoria: Penguin, 1990- . annual); and Robin Bradley's *Australian and New
Zealand wine vintages* ([Melbourne]: Statesman Publication, 1988- . annual).

396   Vineyards of Sydney.
Philip Norrie.   Sydney: Horwitz Grahame, 1990. 222p. maps.
bibliog. tables.

Vines were planted at Sydney Cove soon after the arrival of the First Fleet in 1788. Until
1823 Sydney was the only vineyard region in Australia and it remained the dominant
region for a further thirty years, supplying cuttings for the other new areas developing in
Australia. The book includes official statistics which reveal the significance of the Sydney
region as a wine producing area until, like other Australian vineyards, it was destroyed by
phylloxera at the end of the 19th century. Today, again, there are some ten vineyards in
the Sydney region. The author, a winemaker, presents the history of wine production in
the Sydney area in text and many historic photographs and original drawings.

Literature

General

397 Days of wine and rage.
Frank Moorhouse.   Melbourne: Penguin Books, 1980. 446p.

An anthology of pieces written by the author, a novelist, and others, published in various journals and newspapers. They illustrate the life and thought of the Bohemian counter-culture predominant in Sydney in the 1970s.

398 The sea coast of Bohemia: literary life in Sydney's roaring twenties.
Peter Kirkpatrick.   Brisbane: University of Queensland Press, 1992. 368p. bibliog.

A lively account of Sydney's literary Bohemia of the 1920s. As well as discussing the exploits of the dominant personalities, the author also brings to life 'a large coterie of energetic, intelligent, often eccentric and sometimes outrageous people, most of whom ... have been overlooked or wilfully disregarded by cultural historians'. The book is a valuable addition to Sydney's cultural history, which can also engage the general reader.

399 The Stenhouse circle: literary life in mid-nineteenth century Sydney.
Ann-Mari Jordens.   Melbourne: Melbourne University Press, 1979. 186p.

Nicol Drysdale Stenhouse was Australia's first and probably only important 19th-century literary patron. He dominated the intellectual life of the colony of New South Wales after his emigration from Scotland in the 1840s. His splendid collection of books, which he made freely available to the leading literary figures of the colony, eventually formed the nucleus of Sydney University Library. The book illuminates the intellectual life of 19th-century Sydney and is an important chapter in the cultural history of Australia.

400 Sydney.
In: *The Oxford literary guide to Australia.* General editor Peter
Pierce, for the Association for the Study of Australian Literature.
Melbourne: Oxford University Press, 1993, rev. ed., p. 93-140.

The first literary guide to Australia is now published in a fully revised paperback edition.
The introduction states: 'This book is a celebration of Australian literary landscapes. It is
a record of the many responses writers have made to the natural and constructed sites of
the continent. Entries include towns, townships, suburbs, rivers, mountains and well-
known geographical areas ... and appear alphabetically... The grounds for inclusion are
the biographical and imaginative associations which the authors have formed with these
places. They represent sites from which the writers drew their inspiration, sites where
writers have lived and worked and drunk, have been educated, have married, have died
and are buried'. Forty-seven pages of text are devoted to Sydney, located in the New
South Wales section.

Fiction

401 A city in the mind: Sydney – imagined by its writers.
Edited by Patricia Holt. Sydney: Allen & Unwin, 1983. 131p.
bibliog.

In extracts from their books, twenty-eight novelists reveal how they have portrayed the
city of Sydney in their fiction and autobiographies. A brief biography of each writer,
which places their fiction in its social and temporal context, is accompanied by a portrait
which shows the writer at the time of writing.

402 Sydney's poems.
Edited by Robert Gray, Vivian Smith. Sydney: Primavera, 1992.
76p.

A selection of thirty-eight poems on the occasion of the city's 150th anniversary (1842-
1992).

**403 Botany Bay document: a poetic history of the women of Botany
Bay.**
Jordie Albiston. Melbourne: Black Pepper, 1996. 63p. bibliog.

Using ship log books, legal records, paintings, etchings and maps, newspapers, private
correspondence and diaries, Albiston recreates, in a series of poems, the lives and times
of the first women of the white settlement at Sydney Cove.

404 Beneath the Southern Cross: a novel of Sydney.
Judy Nunn. Sydney: Random House, 1999. 520p. bibliog.

This fictional family saga begins with the arrival in Sydney in 1788 of Thomas Kendall,
a naive nineteen-year-old, transported for the crime of burglary. Besides being a family

chronicle, the novel is a tribute to Sydney and a celebration of the people, who have shaped and continue to shape its character, its skyline and its heart.

405   Wildest dreams.

Michael Wilding.   Brisbane: University of Queensland Press, 1998. 310p.

Michael Wilding holds a personal chair in English and Australian Literature at the University of Sydney and he is the author of a dozen volumes of fiction. This, his latest, presents literary life in Sydney during the 1960s and 1970s through a haze of drugs and alcohol. The narrative is based on the author's experiences of those times and is imbued with irony and humour, allusions and ambiguity. The prose throughout is stylish.

406   Red nights.

Louis Nowra.   Sydney: Pan Macmillan, 1997. 248p.

A novel about Sydney's underworld, written by one of Australia's best-known playwrights. It is a depressing account of the city's high flyers and low-life, depicting a superficial world of respectability where politicians, businessmen and stockbrokers mix with crime bosses and drug barons. The book portrays the emptiness, materialism, the institutionalized corruption and hypocrisy which pervades today's urban life. The inner city, with its Opera House, Harbour Bridge and Circular Quay, provides the backdrop.

407   The Cliff Hardy case files: Wet graves; Beware of the dog; Casino.

Peter Corris.   Sydney: Bantam Books, 1998. 557p.

This is an omnibus edition of three novels set in Sydney, featuring Australia's favourite private investigator, Cliff Hardy. Since *The dying trade* was published in 1980, there have been twenty-two Hardy books. All of them have been acclaimed for their authentic Sydney settings and atmosphere, and the portrayal of Sydney's high and low life. Corris regards Sydney as a 'perfect' city – its beauty, atmosphere and culture providing a spectacular contrast to its under-belly of poverty, corruption and vulgarity. Corris switched to full-time writing after an academic career and has demonstrated a great ability to create credible characters, sustain the flow of dialogue and invent exciting and realistic plots.

408   Amaze your friends.

Peter Doyle.   Sydney: Random House, 1998. 250p.

This novel is set in Sydney's fringe society, the world of men living on the edge of the law, always on the look-out for a quick buck. The book is set in 1959 and portrays the period and its denizens with accuracy and flair. Racily written, with an ear for Australian slang, this is a wild and funny romp through the underside of Sydney from the author of *Get rich quickly,* winner of the 1997 Ned Kelly award for best first crime novel. The author grew up in Sydney and still lives in an inner-city suburb.

409   The Cross.

Mandy Sayer.   Sydney: Angus & Robertson, 1995. 296p.

The author is a rising star in Australian literature. When she was nine, her family was evicted in the course of controversial attempts to redevelop Victoria Street, Kings Cross,

Sydney's inner city Bohemian suburb. She was twelve years old when Juanita Nielson, heiress, newspaper publisher and high-profile green-ban activist, disappeared in mysterious and, to this day, unresolved circumstances. This novel is the fruit of those childhood experiences. The book is written in the form of monologues by ten of the main characters, each of whom presents their view of the dramatic events of the early 1970s. It is a well-written and very entertaining novel. Mandy Sayer has resettled in Kings Cross and wrote the book there.

410 Come in spinner.
Dymphna Cusack, Florence James.   Sydney: Angus & Robertson, 1990. 711p.

An abridged version of this novel was first published in 1951 after it had won the *Daily Telegraph* Australian novel competition. In 1988 the complete edition of *Come in spinner*, reworked by Florence James from the original manuscript, was published. Set in Sydney during the Second World War, the novel vividly portrays the impact of American servicemen on the city and traces the lives of three women who work in a beauty salon of the Hotel South Pacific. The book provides an excellent picture of wartime Sydney and tensions between the 'Yanks' and locals, and the prevailing atmosphere when anything was available for a price. A mini-series for television was produced in 1989.

411 Foveaux.
Kylie Tennant.   Sydney: Angus & Robertson, 1989. 425p.

A lively, humorous novel about the underprivileged and dispossessed inhabitants of the Sydney inner suburb slum Foveaux. The book was first published in 1939. Tennant was born in Sydney in 1912 and knew the city intimately, having lived in several inner city suburbs herself. Three other novels, *Ride on stranger* (1943), *Tell morning this* (1967) and *Tantavalon* (1983), have Sydney settings. Kylie Tennant died in 1988.

412 Harp in the south novels: Missus; The harp in the south; Poor man's orange.
Ruth Park.   Melbourne: Penguin Books, 1986. 684p.

These three popular novels have been brought together in one volume for the first time. Originally published between 1948 and 1985, they depict the fortunes of an Irish-Australian family, the Darcys. Set in the slums of Surry Hills, it is a wonderful, authentic portrayal of inner city life. The works are based on Ruth Park's and her husband's, D'Arcy Niland's, real life experiences. Their joint autobiography, *The drums go bang* (1956), also covers this period as does Ruth Park's second volume of her autobiography *Fishing in the Styx*, published in 1993. The novels have been produced as a mini-series for television.

413 Seven poor men of Sydney.
Christina Stead.   Sydney: Angus & Robertson, 1981. 319p.

This novel, set in the Sydney of the 1920s, was first published in London in 1934. It portrays a group of men and women living in poverty and social turmoil. Set against the vividly drawn background of Fisherman's (Watson's) Bay and the inner Sydney slums, the author concentrates on the diverse emotional lives of the protagonists. The author left Australia in 1928 and wrote many novels while living in Europe and America. She returned to Australia in 1974 and died there in 1983. Her reputation as a novelist has grown steadily over the years.

414 Promised lands.
Jane Rogers.   London: Faber, 1995. 464p.

A critically acclaimed novel in which the author skilfully intertwines the powerful dramas of the first year of the convict colony at Sydney with present-day lives to produce an intelligent and gripping story.

415 The timeless land.
Eleanor Dark.   Sydney: Collins, 1988. 544p.

First published in 1941, this is Dark's first and best known novel in the historical trilogy which traces the first twenty-six years of the white settlement in Australia. *The timeless land* has Sydney as its setting and in the next two volumes, *Storm of time* (1948) and *No barrier* (1953), Sydney remains central. Basing her work on extensive historical research, Dark blends historical figures prominent in early colonial life with fictional characters. The clash of indigenous and European cultures is well portrayed as is the interplay between the various class and group interests in the new society. This is recommended to all readers seeking to understand what life was like in early Sydney. An earlier novel, *Waterway,* published in 1938, is marked by excellent descriptions of its Sydney harbour setting.

416 Pemulwuy: the rainbow warrior.
Eric Willmot.   Sydney: Weldons, 1987. 310p.

This novel, by a prominent member of the Aboriginal community, evokes brilliantly the story of Pemulwuy, a leader of the Eora people, who inhabited the Sydney region when the white man first arrived in 1788. He led his tribe in the resistance against the white invaders for twelve long years until his death in 1802. Until recently Australian history had not even acknowledged the existence of this early guerrilla leader.

Newspapers, Magazines and Journals

417 Yesterday's news: a history of the newspaper press in New South Wales from 1920 to 1945.

R. B. Walker.   Sydney: Sydney University Press, 1980. 243p.

This is the second volume in the author's history of the press in New South Wales. The first volume is entitled *The newspaper press in New South Wales, 1803-1920* (Sydney: Sydney University Press, 1976. 272p.). It is an academic history written by a professional historian and concentrates on the press in Sydney, the state's capital where most of the important newspapers were published.

418 The journalistic javelin: an illustrated history of the Bulletin.

Patricia Rolfe.   Sydney: Wildcat Press, 1979. 314p. bibliog.

A history of the most significant Australian weekly periodical founded in Sydney in 1880 and still published today as a weekly news magazine. The author worked on the *Bulletin* for many years in senior positions. Of special interest are the many cartoons interspersed throughout the text, satirizing Australian and Sydney life over a period of a hundred years.

419 Writers of the Bulletin.

Douglas Stewart.   Sydney: Australian Broadcasting Commission, 1977. 83p. (1977 Boyer Lectures).

A personal memoir of the writers for the periodical, *The Bulletin* by Douglas Stewart, poet, playwright, critic and biographer, who was *The Bulletin*'s literary editor from 1940 to 1960. Another similar book of reminiscences is *Bohemians of The Bulletin* (Sydney: Angus & Robertson, 1973. 160p.), by the famous artist and writer Norman Lindsay who contributed to the magazine since the early 1900s. Writers included are J. F. Archibald, A. G. Stephens, J. H. M. Abbot, A. B. Paterson, James Edmond, Livingston Hopkins, Bernard O'Dowd, Randolph Bedford, Hugh McCrae and Louis Stone.

420 The Archibald paradox: a strange case of authorship.
Sylvia Lawson. Melbourne: Allen Lane, 1983. 292p.

A biography of the publisher of *The Bulletin* magazine, founded in Sydney in 1880, this book is also an analysis of the journal itself and its influence on Australia's colonial culture.

421 Connie Sweetheart: the story of Connie Robertson.
Valerie Lawson. Melbourne: Heinemann, 1990. 349p. bibliog.

Connie Sweetheart Robertson, daughter of the noted literary critic, editor and publisher A. G. Stephens, reached the height of her journalistic career at *The Sydney Morning Herald*. As editor of the women's pages from 1936 to her retirement in 1962, she ruled Sydney's social scene. Details about Connie Robertson's life are scattered rather thinly throughout this biography, which in the first section tells more about her famous father, while the latter part of the book deals with Sydney's social life and the world of journalism. The book is an absorbing study of the recent social history of Sydney, full of interesting characters – writers, journalists, newspaper proprietors, celebrities, socialites and bohemians of the day.

422 Nation: the life of an independent journal of opinion 1958 -1972.
Edited and introduced by K. S. Inglis, assisted by J. Brazier.
Melbourne: Melbourne University Press, 1989. 270p. bibliog.

Nation appeared fortnightly in Sydney from 1958 to 1972. Each issue carried a variety of editorial and contributed articles on politics and the economy, manners and morals, and the arts. It was an influential journal with prominent contributors and the editor, K. S. Inglis, has selected a range of articles for this volume which reflect the flavour of the journal. When *Nation* ceased publication, its name and some of its spirit went into the *Nation Review*.

423 Remember Smith's Weekly? A biography of an uninhibited national Australian newspaper. Born: 1 March 1919. Died 28 October 1950.
George Blaikie. Adelaide: Rigby, 1966. 258p.

An informal, anecdotal account of *Smith's Weekly*, an uninhibited Sydney newspaper. Aggressively nationalistic and somewhat racist, it championed the cause of the returned serviceman or 'digger', extolled the White Australia Policy and was aggressively anti-communist. The author worked as a reporter at *Smith's Weekly* for twenty years until it ceased publication in 1950.

424 Heralds and angels: the house of Fairfax 1841-1992.
Gavin Souter. Melbourne: Penguin Books, 1992. 388p.

The present book updates Souter's *Company of heralds* (1981), a history of John Fairfax Ltd – the oldest publishing company in Australia and the publisher of the *Sydney Morning Herald,* Sydney's main newspaper since 1831, but at the time of writing on the brink of financial ruin. For a racy, journalistic account of the political manoeuvring and frenzy of shady advisers and speculators during the takeover bids for Fairfax, the reader should consult *Corporate cannibals: the taking of Fairfax,* by Coleen Ryan and Glenn Burge

(1992). An earlier account of the takeover battle is *Operation dynasty: how Warwick took John Fairfax Ltd.* by finance journalist Trevor Sykes (1989).

425   The house of Packer: the making of a media empire.

Bridget Griffen-Foley.   Sydney: Allen & Unwin, 1999. 398p. bibliog.

This book is the first major study of the emergence and evolution of one of Australia's largest media empires, Consolidated Press Ltd, publishers of popular magazines and Sydney newspapers the *Daily Telegraph* and the *Sunday Telegraph*. Kerry Packer, Australia's wealthiest man, is at the head of the publishing giant today, but the subject of this book is his father Frank Packer. For better or worse, the House of Packer has made and continues to make a considerable contribution to Australia's public culture. This volume recounts how it all began.

426   The Sydney Morning Herald.

Sydney: John Fairfax, 1831- . daily except Sundays.

The nation's oldest metropolitan daily was founded on 18 April 1831. This and the Melbourne *Age* are the leading newspapers in Australia and carry serious analyses of politics and business, as well as news of Sydney and international affairs and events. The most useful supplements are a television guide on Mondays, a restaurant and food and wine guide called *Good Living* on Tuesdays and an entertainment guide called *Metro* on Fridays. In the Saturday edition an excellent literary supplement is noted for book reviews and art criticism of a high standard. Around 230,000 copies of the *Herald* are sold each day. The thick Saturday edition sells 410,000 copies and contains the classified advertisements that many Sydney people use to seek jobs and buy houses and cars.

427   Daily Telegraph.

Sydney: News Ltd, 1879- . daily.

This tabloid is owned by Rupert Murdoch and sells about 440,000 copies each weekday. Like all tabloids, it caters for popular appeal. The articles are short, the editorial policy, like that of most of its columnists, is conservative and it covers local news, especially crime, in great detail. International coverage restricts itself mainly to show business. Its sister paper, *The Sunday Telegraph,* is Australia's biggest-selling newspaper at over 710,000 copies a week.

428   Over one hundred & fifteen years of news from the archives of The Sydney Daily Telegraph, Daily Pictorial, Daily Telegraph, Sydney Daily Mirror, The Daily Telegraph Mirror.

Written and compiled by Christopher Wright.   Sydney: Adrian Savvas, 1995. unpaginated.

This large-format book presents the story of the *Sydney Daily Telegraph,* since it was first published in 1879, through the author's comments and reproductions of the newspaper's front pages. It gives an idea of the nature and editorial slant of Sydney's second-longest running newspaper.

Libraries, Art Galleries and Museums

429 Sydney museums guide: over 120 museums & collections of everything.
Peta Landman, Michael Bogle.   Sydney: Kingsclear Books, 1993.
85p.

Over 120 museums and collections in Sydney are listed in alphabetical order with subject and geographical indexes. Each entry describes the museum, and comments on highlights, opening times, access to public transport facilities, children's activities, handicapped access and special activities. It is an invaluable guidebook for tourists, visitors, Sydneysiders, teachers and parents.

430 Portrait of a gallery.
Edited by Edmund Capon, Jan Meek.   Sydney: Trustees of the Art Gallery of New South Wales, 1984. 131p.

Spectacularly situated in parkland on the edge of the Sydney Central Business District, the Art Gallery of New South Wales dates from 1871. Edmund Capon, its Director, expresses the aims of this handsome, profusely illustrated volume, in the following words: 'This book is not devoted specifically to the collections of the Art Gallery of New South Wales, nor is it specifically devoted to the building that houses those collections. It is a book about the Gallery, how and why it functions, its more prized possessions, its seen and unseen activities, the events, exhibitions and works of art – in fact all the ingredients which contribute to its special and distinctive character'. The book achieves these aims admirably.

431 Treasures of the State Library of New South Wales: the Australian collections.
Anne Robertson.   Sydney: Collins in association with the State Library of New South Wales, 1988. 194p. bibliog.

Produced to coincide with the opening of the new State Library complex in 1988, this lavish volume outlines the Australiana holdings of the Library. The text contains brief biographies of two major donors, David Scott Mitchell and Sir William Dixson, and articles on selected items in the collections of pictures, manuscripts, printed material and maps and charts, which are held in both the Mitchell Library and the Dixson Library and Galleries. There are also sections on coins, medals and stamps, bookplates and relics. Many illustrations are in colour. The author worked in the Library for thirty years in various senior positions.

432 Rare and curious specimens: an illustrated history of the Australian Museum 1827-1979.

Ronald Strahan and others.   Sydney: The Australian Museum, 1979. 173p.

The Australian Museum in Sydney is the oldest museum in the country, dating from 1827. It is considered to be one of the best natural history museums in the world and is visited by nearly one million people every year. The collections cover the fields of anthropology, geology, palaeontology and the natural sciences, with the exception of botany. It provides educational services and has an active display policy, new exhibitions being completed every year. This large-format, illustrated book was produced as part of the celebrations of the 150th anniversary of the institution in 1977. The several expert contributors deal with the history of the museum and its collections.

433 Discovering the Powerhouse Museum: a personal view.

Terence Measham.   Sydney: The Beagle Press for Powerhouse Publishing, 1997. 200p. bibliog.

In 1988 Australia's largest museum, the Powerhouse, opened its doors to the public in Sydney. Its history, however, dates back to 1879 and the Sydney International Exhibition, when what is now called the Museum of Applied Arts and Sciences, or Powerhouse, began its collections. This large-format, lavishly illustrated volume by the Museum's director is a sequel to *Treasures of the Powerhouse Museum* (Haymarket, New South Wales: Powerhouse Publishing, 1994. 192p.). Like its predecessor, this book reveals many of the objects at the museum in full-colour photographs. However, it is different in scope as it provides a lively discussion of how and why the Powerhouse exhibits as it does. A visit to the Powerhouse should be on the itinerary of all visitors to Sydney and either of these books provides a spectacular introduction and memoir to the holdings of the museum.

434 Mr Macleay's celebrated cabinet: the history of the Macleays and their museum.

Edited by Peter Stanbury, Julian Holland.   Sydney: The Macleay Museum, The University of Sydney, 1988. 171p.

The Macleay Museum at the University of Sydney consists of natural history collections assembled by the Macleay family in the late 18th and 19th centuries. This book celebrates the Museum's centenary in 1988 and explains the history of the acquisition of the collections.

435 Sydney Jewish Museum: a museum of Australian Jewish history and the Holocaust.
Sydney: The Museum, 1994. 64p.

This well-illustrated publication marks the opening of the Museum on 18 November 1992. The exhibits deal with Jewish life, from the time of the sixteen Jewish convicts who arrived on the First Fleet until the present day, and also depicts graphically the fate of Jews during the Holocaust.

Reference Works

436   The Australian encyclopaedia.
Sydney: Australian Geographic Society, 1996. 6th ed. 8 vols.

The latest edition of the *Australian encyclopaedia* has been completely reset, redesigned, substantially revised, freshly illustrated and contains the largest number of words so far. The eighth volume comprises a statistical appendix and a comprehensive index, through which Sydney entries can be traced. People and places are featured in the alphabetical sequence. Some fundamental articles in earlier editions, especially the second, published in 1953, retain their intrinsic value.

437   Australian dictionary of biography.
Melbourne: Melbourne University Press, 1966- . 14 vols to date.

The largest and most scholarly source of Australian biographical information is complete to 1939 in twelve volumes. The thirteenth and fourteenth volumes, published in 1993 and 1996 respectively, cover the years 1940-80, A–Kel. When volumes fifteen and sixteen have been completed, work will begin on the period 1981-90. People connected with Sydney can be found under their surnames in the alphabetical sequence. There is an index volume to volumes one to twelve, which contains a listing of names according to the main occupations of the biographees, and another listing according to place of birth. Living persons are listed in *Who's who in Australia* (see following entry).

438   Who's who in Australia: an Australian biographical dictionary and register of prominent people with which is incorporated Johns's notable Australians (first issued 1906).
Melbourne: Information Australia Group, 1906- . annual.

Lists prominent Australians, including many Sydney residents. Details about careers, hobbies and recreational pursuits and addresses are supplied with each entry. *The Australian dictionary of biography* (see preceding item) lists people who have died. The latest (35th) edition of *Who's who in Australia* was published in 1999.

439 Australian autobiographical narratives: an annotated bibliography.
Kay Walsh, Joy Hooton.   Canberra: Australian Scholarly Editions Centre, University College, UNSW, Australian Defence Force Academy and National Library of Australia, 1993-98. 2 vols.

Volume one covers the period up to 1850 and volume two, the period 1850-1900. Sydney autobiographies are listed in the place index under Sydney. There are ninety-one autobiographies of Sydney interest in the first volume and sixty-eight entries in the second volume. These autobiographies throw much light on life in Sydney during its first 112 years. There are lengthy summaries of the content of the autobiographies. As well as the place index, there are also name and detailed subject indexes.

440 Family and local history sources in the Sydney area.
Compiled and edited by Jennie Fairs, Dom Meadley.   Melbourne: Meadley Family History Services, 1995. 133p. bibliog.

The purpose of this book is to provide a survey of the records relating to family history, local history, social history and biography available in Sydney and to give their location and the means of gaining access to them. In effect, it is a directory of archives, repositories, libraries, museums, historical societies and cemeteries, with detailed descriptions of their holdings. There is also an extensive bibliography.

441 Bibliography of New South Wales local history: an annotated bibliography of secondary works published before 1982.
Christine Eslick, Joy Hughes, R. Ian Jack.   Sydney: NSWU Press, 1987. 435p.

This major bibliography of local histories and directories contains nearly 2,600 items, including journal articles, and is divided into metropolitan Sydney and country areas. There are useful cross-references and an index of subjects, authors, compilers and editors. The work also contains *New South Wales directories 1828-1950: a bibliography* by Joy Hughes.

Indexes

There follow three separate indexes: authors (personal or corporate); titles; and subjects. Title entries are italicized and refer either to the main titles, or to other works cited in the annotations. The numbers refer to bibliographical entry rather than page number. Individual index entries are arranged in alphabetical sequence.

Index of Authors

Caplan, S. 168
Capon, E. 430
Carbery, G. 182
Cardew, R. V. 264
Carew, E. 261
Carey, H. M. 173
Carolan, A. 130
Carroll, B. 273
Carruthers, S. L. 123
Carter, P. 163
Cashman, R. 130, 371, 375
Castillo, A. 164
Castles, A. 243
Champion, R. 3
Chapman, D. 108
Chippendale, P. 210
Christie, M. 250
Clegg, J. 162
Cleverley, J. F. 205
Clifford, L. 48
Clune, F. 12, 247
Clyne, D. 149
Cobley, J. 103
Coffey, R. 325
Colless, S. 343
Collingwood, J. 40
Collins, D. 105
Collins, J. 164
Collins, T. 307
Coltheart, L. 326
Connell, R. W. 233
Connell, W. F. 210
Coombs, A. 178
Cope, I. 199
Corbyn, C. A. 248
Corris, P. 407
Cotton, L. 246
Coward, D. 285
Cox, I. C. 156
Cripps, A. J. 358
Crittenden, V. 110
Crocker, J. 40
Crocker, R. 93
Crowe, D. 52
Cumes, J. W. C. 372
Cumpston, J. S. 282

Curson, P. 193
Curson, P. H. 191
Cusack, D. 80, 410
Cutler, M. 382

D

Dale, D. 7
Dalton, R. 77
Daly, M. T. 263
Daniel, G. 51
Dark, E. 415
Davidson, J. 8
Davidson, L. 83
Davies, S. 64
Davis, Q. 11
Davis, Q. F. 30
De Marco, C. 309
de Vries-Evans, S. 28
Derriman, P. 376
Docker, J. 9
Dow, G. M. 258
Doyle, P. 408
Drew, P. 320-21
Drewe, R. 10, 127
Duncan, K. 19
Dunstan, K. 10
Dupain, M. 301, 323, 337-38
Dupleix, J. 392
Durack, T. 392
Dutton, G. 10, 27, 345
Dyster, B. 271

E

Earnshaw, B. 83
Edmonds, T. 145
Egan, J. 102
Egloff, B. 327
Elder, B. 45
Eldershaw, F. 101
Eldershaw, M. B. 101
Ellis, M. H. 117
Ellyard, D. 322
Emanuel, C. 24, 27, 32

Eslick, C. 441
Evans, I. 338
Evatt, H. V. 117

F

Fairley, A. 51, 146
Fairs, J. 440
Ferguson, J. 10, 387
Fielding-Jones Dupree, A. 224
Fitton, D. 360
Fitzgerald, A. 10
Fitzgerald, P. 284
Fitzgerald, R. 117
Fitzgerald, S. 87, 98, 128-29, 132, 165-66, 228
Fitzhardinge, L. F. 104
Flannery, T. 104
Fletcher, B. 106
Fletcher, B. H. 105, 212, 255
Fletcher, J. 204
Flynn, M. 109, 111
Foley, J. D. 195
Ford, J. 367
Formica, J. 340
Forrest, J. 188
Fowles, J. 306
Frame, T. R. 65
Franki, G. 203
Fraser, D. 313
Freeland, J. M. 337
Freney, D. 79
Freud, S. 382

G

Gaby, J. 267
Gall, J. 283
Garrett, W. 199
Garton, S. 194
Geeves, P. 31-32
Gibbs, S. 375
Gibson, J. B. 202
Gilbert, L. 148
Gill, L. 13

Gillen, M. 109
Gillett, R. 281
Goddard, R. H. 190
Golder, H. 128, 229
Gollings, J. 342
Gould, F. 232
Gowing, S. 252
Grabosky, P. N. 235
Grace, H. 177
Gray, R. 402
Greenfield, J. 265
Greenland, H. 230
Griffen-Foley, B. 425
Griffith, K. 151

H

Hainsworth, D. R. 262
Hall, G. 15
Hall, H. 358
Hall, R. 58
Halliday, J. 395
Halliday, R. W. 203
Hamilton, D. G. 200
Haskell, J. 293
Heads, I. 378-79
Healy, G. 125
Hearn, M. 117
Henry, F. J. J. 317
Herman, M. 299, 306
Hickie, D. 237, 242, 374
Hickie, T. V. 377, 381
Hindwood, K. A. 150
Hole, W. V. 81, 216
Holland, G. 214
Holland, J. 434
Holt, P. 401
Hooke, H. 395
Hooton, J. 439
Hordern, L. 76
Horne, D. 72
Hoskin, E. S. 150
Howard, R. 57
Howe, G. 385
Howell, J. 144
Hubble, A. 364

Huber, R. 169
Hudson, L. C. 190
Hughes, A. 371
Hughes, J. 83, 116, 304, 337, 441
Hutchinson, M. 220

I

Inglis, K. S. 422
Innes, D. J. 383
Irvin, E. 298, 357
Irving, R. 301
Isaacs, E. 170
Ivory, H. 333

J

Jack, R. I. 218, 441
Jahn, G. 294
James, F. 410
Jenkins, D. 123
Jeremy, J. 253
Jervis, J. 141
Johansen, A. 202
Johnson, A. 18
Johnson, C. 296
Johnson, H. 347
Johnson, L. 120
Johnston, C. 179
Jones, D. J. 330
Jones, M. 137
Jordens, A. M. 399
Judd, S. 172

K

Kabos, A. 336
Kades, C. 340
Kalajzich, P. 290
Karskens, G. 95-96, 140
Kass, T. 141
Keane, E. 366
Keating, C. 129, 131, 143
Kelly, M. 93, 95, 115, 122, 126, 134, 184, 193

Keneally, T. 71
Kennedy, B. 59, 125, 219, 315
Kennedy, L. 240
Kennedy, R. 181
Kenny, J. 156
Kent, W. 22
Kingsmill, J. 4, 75
Kingston, D. 303
Kinstler, J. 301
Kirkpatrick, P. 74, 398
Knox, P. 53
Kohen, J. 159
Kohen, J. L. 160
Korporaal, G. 370
Kyle, N. 208

L

Landman, P. 429
Lang, M. 139
Langdale, J. V. 264
Larcombe, F. A. 227, 231
Lawrence, J. 49
Lawson, S. 420
Lawson, V. 239, 421
Leplastrier, R. 340
Liddle, D. 133
Lind, L. 123
Linge, G. J. R. 249
Liston, C. 141
Little, G. 257
Lord, S. 51
Lucas, C. 338
Lynch, W. B. 231

M

McBryde, I. 158
McCarter, G. 6
McClymont, J. 141
McCormick, T. 92
McCoy, A. W. 236
Mc Cracken, K. 193
McFarlane, J. 33
McGeoch, R. 370

Index of Titles

O

P

Q

R

Index of Subjects

A

Aborigines
antiquities 89
art 162
artefacts 161, 163
biographies 156-57
contacts with Europeans
101, 103-05, 155-58,
161
culture 154, 159, 161
depiction in art 157, 161,
355
education 160
fiction 416
genealogy 159
government relations
155, 158
guidebooks 162
history 154-55, 158, 163
illustrations 154, 156-58,
161
languages 163
Russian attitudes 161
treatment 155-58, 160
vocabularies 159
Western Sydney 159-60
Actresses
biographies 360
Aerial photographs 15, 18,
57
Agricultural exhibitions
history 255
illustrations 255
Airports
environmental aspects
284
history 283-84
location 284
political aspects 284

Allen, Allen & Hemsley
(law firm) 239
Allen, George (1800-77)
84
Anderson, John (1893-
1962) 178, 219
Anderson, Maybanke
(1845-1927) 82
Anglican Church
history 172
Annandale
history 135
illustrations 135
social conditions 135
social life and customs
135
Arcades
history 334
illustrations 334
Archaeological
excavations 89, 96, 327
Archibald, Jules Francois
(1856-1910) 420
Architects
biographies 294, 296,
319-21, 336-38, 340
Architecture
and the physically
handicapped 55
colonial 184, 296, 299-
306, 337-38
designs and plans 298
domestic 301-05, 336,
341
Glebe 305
guidebooks 293-95
history 90, 116, 296,
297-300
modern 229, 295, 319-21
organic 340

Archives
directories 440
Arson 270
Art
Aboriginal 162
collections 348-50
depiction in 4, 24-25, 27-
29, 32, 62, 91-92,
355-56
exhibitions 347, 351
history 345-47, 351-56
modern 345, 351, 354
19th century 91-92,
352
patronage 346-47, 353
Art critics
biographies 73
Art dealers
biographies 351, 353
Art galleries
history 347-49, 351, 353
Art Gallery of New South
Wales
collections 348, 430
history 347-48, 430
Art museums 347-50, 430
Art patrons
biographies 346, 353
Art publishing 346
Art societies
history 347
Artists
biographies 356
Artists camps
Mosman 352
Arts
decorative 349-50
19th century 116
Ascham School
history 224

147

Sydney City Centre

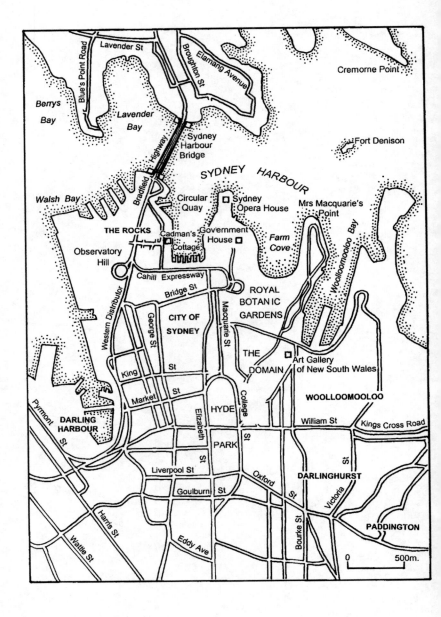

Sydney and Its Region

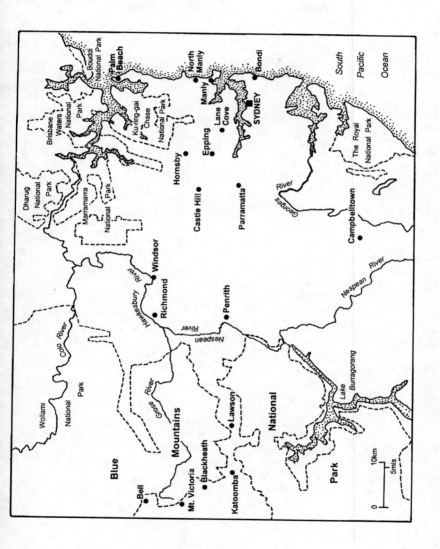

ALSO FROM CLIO PRESS

INTERNATIONAL ORGANIZATIONS SERIES

Each volume in the International Organizations Series is either devoted to one specific organization, or to a number of different organizations operating in a particular region, or engaged in a specific field of activity. The scope of the series is wide ranging and includes intergovernmental organizations, international non-governmental organizations, and national bodies dealing with international issues. The series is aimed mainly at the English-speaker and each volume provides a selective, annotated, critical bibliography of the organization, or organizations, concerned. The bibliographies cover books, articles, pamphlets, directories, databases and theses and, wherever possible, attention is focused on material about the organizations rather than on the organizations' own publications. Notwithstanding this, the most important official publications, and guides to those publications, will be included. The views expressed in individual volumes, however, are not necessarily those of the publishers.

VOLUMES IN THE SERIES

1 *European Communities*, John Paxton
2 *Arab Regional Organizations*, Frank A. Clements
3 *Comecon: The Rise and Fall of an International Socialist Organization*, Jenny Brine
4 *International Monetary Fund*, Anne C. M. Salda
5 *The Commonwealth*, Patricia M. Larby and Harry Hannam
6 *The French Secret Services*, Martyn Cornick and Peter Morris
7 *Organization of African Unity*, Gordon Harris
8 *North Atlantic Treaty Organization*, Phil Williams
9 *World Bank*, Anne C. M. Salda
10 *United Nations System*, Jospeh P. Baratta
11 *Organization of American States*, David Sheinin
12 *The British Secret Services*, Philip H. J. Davies
13 *The Israeli Secret Services*, Frank A. Clements